DNA

Beyond The Physical

Dictation from The Great White Brotherhood

Bob Sanders

DISCLAIMERS

This is a free eBook. You are encouraged to share it for free (in unmodified form) to whomever you wish. If you have paid for this eBook, you should request or seek an immediate refund.

The author has made every effort to ensure that the accuracy of the information within this book was correct at time of publication. The author does not assume and hereby disclaims any liability to any party for any loss, damage, or disruption caused by errors or omissions, whether such errors or omissions result from accident, negligence, or any other cause.

COPYRIGHT

This book was authored by Bob Sanders and dictated to him from The Great White Brotherhood by clairaudience, or as some people call "channelling". It is free for everyone to read and share unmodified for spiritual advancement. Please share this book unmodified with anyone and anywhere you can to help spread the messages it contains. For more information please visit the following internet sites:

https://www.thegreatwhitebrotherhood.org

https://www.thestairwaytofreedom.orghttps://www.youtube.com/channel/UC2UDv0r4mtNPEWbve5YHDeg/

First edition – September 2018

Cover Artwork by Paul Saunders

Author – Bob Sanders

ISBN: 9781723918063
Imprint: Independently published

TABLE OF CONTENTS

FOREWORD 5
CHAPTER 1 7
CHAPTER 2 13
CHAPTER 3 22
CHAPTER 4 34
CHAPTER 5 45
CHAPTER 6 54
CHAPTER 7 65
CHAPTER 8 74
CHAPTER 9 87

FOREWORD

This book will be the sixth in this series, that discusses some of the many aspects of life, which is not only endless but covers unimaginable aspects of creation that goes on, not only beyond what we have already covered in the previous volumes but, ultimately, would take us on to levels far beyond the comprehension of any of you and, it must be said, beyond the comprehension of any of us.

One could ask the question, of course, that as all life only exists in the degree that comprehension allows, if we get to the point where the comprehension of even the wisest of us will not exceed, could life still continue?

From a certain point, a certain aspect, we could say that life does not go beyond comprehension - and that would be true - nevertheless, at some point in the future, consciousness will expand and, at that point, existence will expand to fill the gap created by expanded consciousness.

Life hates a void, a vacuum and, although we have said that in reality nothing exists and it is all imagination; illusion creating a sort of reality, we must admit that what we described as all of existence not really existing in any tangible form, what we were really admitting was that we had no means of comprehending the next level and that we described it all as "nothing".
No time, no space, no planets, no gravity - in effect - no life, but this concept we called God, we must now admit that, of course, it was not true.
It was just an excuse for not going any deeper.

It is also true that, although we suspect that life goes on endlessly, there does come a point where our level of understanding ends and, at that point, we just have a blank.
But that does not mean that there is nothing beyond that point. It just means that we have no means of reaching into that void.
But we are not quite at that moment yet.

We feel the need to apologise to you for not always telling you the truth concerning life (existence) but we have done it for a good reason and, no doubt, will do so again.

If and when we are discussing a complicated subject, we do not want your minds, individually and collectively, to stray from the subject under discussion and, we must also say that many of you will have had no knowledge of what we have discussed in these various other books.

If you go back to when we first started to give you information and if you have followed attentively the information that we have revealed to you, you will admit, we hope, that we have all taken great strides in many areas.

But we have to reveal existence to you slowly and carefully, to lead you into these difficult concepts.

Even now, as we start book 6 in this series, you may well be wondering what on Earth - or heaven - is left to discuss but we can assure you that the living library (the Akashic Record) is stocked with information and goes into areas that no human, incarnate or discarnate could comprehend.

Into those areas there would be no point in venturing.
Words do not exist to describe some aspects of life and you would have no ability to comprehend if we tried.

But in this book, Volume 6, we intend to try to explain the concept behind DNA, in as full a manner as possible.

We know that we have touched on this subject a number of times but, DNA is a quite complicated topic and requires a serious study to move beyond the level of comprehension that man has today and, in fact, links with many - indeed most - of the subjects that the other books discussed.

It is quite amazing that the subject of "existence", with all its ramifications, can be made to sound cold, lifeless and boring by scientists, but we hope that you, who have followed our other books, have found our explanations interesting.
So, let us turn to DNA and recount, briefly, the history of its discovery.

CHAPTER 1

DNA – INTRODUCTION & HISTORY

As far as modern history is concerned, the study of DNA started just after the end of World War II, when some scientists managed to discover physical evidence of what is referred to as the "double helix", a rather technical way of describing the simple building blocks of life.

Eventually, these findings were revealed to the world and progress has been made in being able to identify many tissue or blood samples and compare them to known other samples, thus permitting to identify a previously unidentified sample.

This is considered important to modern man and many criminal cases have been resolved one way or another to the satisfaction of the legal authorities of various countries.

Identification of various other animal and plant specimens have also been made, so the discovery of DNA is considered to be a very important point. And so, it is.

The problem is, of course, to discover why DNA exists because, if it does exist, it must have been created by the various Archangelic beings that put into motion the wishes of God and so there must be a reason for DNA above and beyond solving a few crimes - which could easily be done by entering the Akashic Record and watching any crime unfold, because it is all faithfully recorded in the Akashic Record.

Another question that one might ask is, if there were very advanced races that lived on Earth long ago, did they make use of being able to understand and manipulate DNA in their various experiments?

Further, we might well ask that, if it is true that the non-physical exists and is by far the most important part of man, what role does DNA play in the non-physical realms?

We might go on and question just how far up through the dimensions does DNA, in astral form, go, at what point is it added to the Logos of man and then go on to establish its future role in the development of life?

You can see that we can ask a number of questions concerning DNA that take us far outside of the field of identification of blood and tissue samples.

We will say at this point that DNA is a fundamental aspect of creation, that everything has DNA and, had it not been thought of by the Directors Of Life, life as we know it could not be.
It is one of the most important aspects of life and is, possibly, second only to the placing of the Logos in living matter.

It is considered to be the key that unlocks all of creation in all dimensions.

Now, we could end this short introductory explanation of DNA and move on to describing its various attributes, some of which we questioned above, but while we are in this introductory chapter, let us step back to the distant past and try to describe the race that first discovered DNA, amongst many things, because this is the same advanced race that we mentioned in the last book and that we said contributed to the creation of UFOs and PLF.

Much of what is discovered today has its roots in this ancient civilisation and it is the record of their many inventions and discoveries, all carefully stored in the Akashic Record, that enables modern man to progress.

The Akashic Record is called a living library, as we have often mentioned, and part of its life aspect constantly broadcasts out in time and in all dimensions, information rather like a TV station constantly broadcasting its archives to the world.

So, by the Law of Mutual Attraction, modern man reaches out with his mind and seeks answers to questions.
These questions are picked up by the Akashic Record and, in certain circumstances, when modern man is ready, he can link with that part of the Akashic Record that is broadcasting the information he seeks and then the person get flashes of information - moments of clarity - when he suddenly knows the answer to a problem.

So, it is largely thanks to this ancient race that made so many advances, all of which are stored in the Akashic Record, that man progresses today.

As we said that this chapter would be about the history of the discovery of DNA, in all fairness, we will say that this ancient race was the first to discover and quantify DNA as far as we are aware.

We perhaps ought to say that life actually is endless and when one cycle finishes, everything disappears and then restarts from zero and so, no doubt, DNA has been discovered countless times but as these previous cycles of life have no relevance to us today, we should remain within the history of existence as we know it - or at least as far as is contained in the Akashic Record, including the restricted area we mentioned in another book.

It is worth taking a moment examining this ancient race, because they played a great role in Earth's history over a long period of time.

There is no point in talking about when they lived and where.
First, it is such a long time ago, that this race has almost no relevance to us and also planet Earth has greatly altered over these vast distances of time, so it would be pointless in talking about geography.

But this race did exist, went through all the teething troubles that all civilisations go through, including at least one total swing of the pendulum of life into darkness and then into light, and the Akashic Record contains much information relevant to this group.

So, what can we say about them?
Perhaps, for those who have not studied the various books and essays that we have provided you with to give you an understanding of life on Earth - and human life in particular - we should mention that life has always gone through the four cycles that all life goes through; birth, growth, decline and death (as far as physicality is concerned).

This may be a not too strange concept to think that you who read this book may well, and inevitably, go through that four-fold cycle, but it is difficult to imagine that the human race is also similarly fated.

We are taught by history that the human race came from "somewhere", developed into what it is today, but it is more difficult to imagine that, at some point, the entire human race will start to decline and will then die out.

We seldom consider these last two aspects of life but, as we have already explained, all life is one and if a May fly eventually dies, the entire human race will cease to exist at some point in the future.
But, for those of you who are starting to get anxious, don't worry!
Our predictions show a long and glorious future.
So, we are talking about many millions - possibly billions - of years into the future, by which time, no doubt, some other life form will be there to take over from us humans, rather like mammals were developed to replace the dinosaurs once the necessity for them being on Earth had outlived its usefulness.

But to return to this ancient race, they did exist, they did thrive for a long time and they did make wonderful scientific and sociological advances.

There is one aspect of the last two parts to life that always has a certain unpredictability. A person, for example, is born, he starts to grow and we know that at some point he will die - or his physical body will. The rest of him is immortal.

But he may live for long years, in which case he will start to decline and, eventually, his body, being no longer able to carry the "weight" of his existence, ceases to function and we say that the person has died.
In fact, as you should know, he has merely changed dimensions and will continue in the astral realms.

But this series of events does not always follow quite in that fashion.
The human body is fragile and so a number of things can cause the demise of the person without him passing through the "decline" part.

So, we might just have birth, growth (either for a few minutes or a relatively few years) and then, in the prime of his life, death ensues.

This can happen to anything, large or small.

In the case of this race that we mentioned, humanity was born - created if you wish - grew for a long period of time and was then eliminated by an ELE, a comet hitting the Earth with sufficient force to cause total elimination of all life (or most of it). Certainly, the vast majority of these humans were eliminated. However, a few survived, moved underground and their descendants are alive to this day.

We know them as the Tall Whites. What they call themselves is not important.

All we need to know today about them is that they are noble, highly intelligent, peaceful beings that live quietly on planet Earth.

We would not know about them at all, except for the fact that man developed the atomic bomb and these Tall Whites met with Earth's representatives to advise man to put a stop to nuclear proliferation - advice that was not taken.
The rest, as they say, is history!

But this previous race were tall and, despite the name they now carry, had many skin colours, as does today's surface population of Earth.
They had developed long past any form of racism.

They understood far more about Prime Creator than the average person does today and had outgrown religion.

There was plenty for all, so there was no need of any war - which still rocks planet Earth today because of all the thoughts of separatism created by race, religion and political division.

They lived and still live (those that still exist) in peace together.
Crime was virtually unknown.
Fear was unknown.

However, it must be understood that this race lived for a long time and so had lived through terrible times that occurred when the pendulum swing of destiny was in the negative cycle.

Thanks to experience gained during the negative cycle, once life swung into positivity, they quickly adopted a peaceful, positive attitude to all life.

From the point of view of science, they developed many aspects of investigation, mostly for peaceful purposes, that enabled them to advance in degrees that aided all of the Earth's population; human, animal, plant and even mineral.

They understood the oneness of all life and, as they lived in peace as one family, had no need of weapons of destruction, although their records do contain memories of arms created when in the negative cycles.

As we mentioned in the last book, they developed spaceships, which enabled them to travel quickly around the planet and even to other planets, although they did not harm any of the other planets.
They went into space as peaceful visitors, for the pleasure of exploration, not that there is much to see on other planets, as they contain no life.

They developed the ability of changing dimensions and could communicate telepathically, although they could also communicate verbally and had written language.

But our main interest at the moment, with this group, is genetics.
Understanding genetics requires an understanding of DNA.
Once they had moved into the positive swing of the galactic pendulum, any experiments that were conducted were done exclusively to assist all life but we must mention that this race, when in the negative cycle, did conduct genetic experiments on animals and humans, the results of which are carried down to us today in mythology and which are being copied by Earth scientists today.

So, we could say that they had a relative mastery of DNA, certainly enough to modify animals and humans.
And certainly, later, to correct any defaults that might appear in a person or animal that impeded it from obtaining its full potential.

But nothing lasts forever and so, unfortunately, an ELE wiped out most of this race.

Whether this was a good or a bad thing is not our concern but we will say that had they continued until today, life would be greatly different from what it is.

After all, since that distant time, we have gone through other swings of the pendulum of life, both positive and negative and one shudders to think what an extremely advanced race, held in the grips of evil, might have accomplished.
But, it is all hypothetical and we go on from where we find ourselves today.

So, we would like to say that much information about DNA is contained in the archives of the Akashic Record although, until this version of life fully exits the negative pull of the pendulum of life, perhaps it is just as well that today's scientists do not, generally, have the ability to access the Akashic Record.

We will also say that, generally, demonic forces do not have that ability either, which protects all life from the harm these demonic forces would cause if they could stand on the shoulders of scientific giants from the past, whose great strides are all faithfully recorded in the Akashic Record.

It is not that the Akashic Record is protected from evil forces - it is open to all. But it is a spiritual concept and requires a certain degree of positivity before one can rise to the level of where the Akashic Record is and thus link with it.

We do not criticize these negative forces; they are necessary to the balance of life, but we must say that negativity (we can't really call it evil, although it appears so sometimes) is by its very nature not conducive to productivity and so, if the demonic forces had access to the Akashic Record, they would scour it to find ever-increasing ways of causing chaos. As it is, until we fully move into the light, they cause enough harm.
But their actions are reducing and will do so increasingly as we move further and further into the light.

We will also mention that this lack of spirituality is also hampering many of today's scientists from being influenced by the Akashic Record.
As we mentioned, the Akashic Record is constantly broadcasting its information out in a multifaceted fashion and, if today's scientists were more spiritual in nature, they would be able to open themselves more to influence by the Akashic Record.

But thanks to the Archon influence, science and religion have divorced themselves from a belief in Prime Creator and the average scientist proudly states that he is an atheist, which seems strange when we consider that every aspect of him, every atom, every molecule in all the dimensions that he consists of, contains nothing but this life force that we refer to as God and which some call Prime Creator.

The very thing that he denies having any belief in is actually the totality of all that he consists of.

With regard to religion, we have often stated that religions exist to enslave people to perpetuate those religions.
Any real spiritual help they give people is more by accident than design.
Please do not think we are criticizing any individual dignitary or layman.
We are suggesting that the concept of religion has strayed from what was first intended by people like the Master Jesus; simple prayer and help groups.

However, we are straying from the subject of DNA.
We wish, in closing this chapter, to say that we may, from time to time, wander from a strict analysis of DNA, because DNA is closely linked to virtually all aspects of all life in all dimensions.

Therefore, as we proceed with this book, if we feel, for you to comprehend some aspect of DNA, the need to explain a subset, we will, but rest assured that we will do our best to stay as focused on DNA - the subject of this book - as possible.

CHAPTER 2

DNA FROM A PHYSICAL PERSPECTIVE

Let us try to examine what is known about DNA from a physical standpoint.

We will not be using any scientific terms. These rather obscure words used by doctors, chemists and various other people who work in scientific fields are all well and good for them. They are a sort of shorthand and avoid any confusion when describing an event, condition or aspect of anatomy but we are interested in explaining complicated matters to lay people, who may well have only a limited knowledge of medical terminology.

So, just what is DNA?
It is described as a double helix.
This means that there are two strands of some material and, between the two strands are a number of connecting points.
The easiest way to understand this is to imagine a ladder.
The two strands are the outside poles (side rails) of the ladder and the connecting points are the rungs that a person would climb up and down in a real ladder.

The main difference in the analogy is that with DNA, the concept twists rather like a spiral staircase, whereas a ladder tends to be straight.

So, this was the image first presented to science.

This was such an exciting discovery that it was some time before chemists and those interested in the subject of DNA started to ask the question… why?

Why does DNA exist?
Why are there two strands, connected, instead of just one or instead of 200?
What is the significance of DNA?

Then it was discovered that each and every person has a unique form of DNA.

As chemists started to compare the DNA of different people and animals, it was realised that there was a remarkable similarity between some animals and humans.
Some DNA aspects are so similar that it was hard to tell creatures apart. Hard to tell some animal life forms from humans.

This caused some consternation, because it was realised that physical humans are almost identical - from a DNA point of view - to many animals.
Humans are not the remote, superior force that has exploited most animals in one way or another.

Many animals, it was realised, are closely related to humans, so close as to be almost the same from a DNA point of view.

One would have thought that this realization would have been enough to stop man from exploiting and eating animals that are closely related to humans.
Cousins one might almost say.
But no! Humanity turns a blind eye to that and carries on eating them.
This, to us, suggests almost a form of cannibalism, although we must, in all honesty, admit that many of us in the Great White Brotherhood, when in incarnation, were ignorant of the close connection between man and beast and consumed them out of that ignorance.

We know better now and, if ever we had our lives over again, but were armed with the knowledge that we now have, we would be strictly vegan.

Quite apart from the physical pain and suffering inflicted on the animal kingdom by this barbaric practice, quite apart from the illnesses provoked in humans by the consumption of animal flesh, when one realizes that one is consuming a creature virtually identical in DNA terms to oneself, it does make one realised that man has not really advanced much over the years that separate him from the earliest creatures that walked the Earth.
One could use the excuse that until DNA was discovered, the connection between man and animals was unknown but who, today, in "civilized" realms, does not know of the close connection between man and a whole variety of animals.

Just because their physical shape may not resemble a person, we ought to have the intelligence to realize that we are closely related to the animal kingdom.

After all, there are a whole variety of animals that have a body, two legs, two "arms", a head exactly as man does.
The fact that they walk on all fours and are covered in fur, makes them appear much different but they have basically the same attributes that man has and now we know the connection through DNA, one should realize that enough is enough.

But, all too often this close connection has been a source of ribaldry, of jokes, of laughter and man continues to consume his cousin.

But, behind this apparent error of nature, that has made the mistake of linking the DNA of man to that of animals, we must realize that nature seldom makes mistakes and never of such proportions.

Therefore, if the DNA of man and the animal kingdom demonstrates a close connection, that connection must exist, despite every effort by religions to prove man's superiority over animals.
Science, in this case, tends to remain fairly neutral on the subject and contents itself in demonstrating this close connection, without getting involved in any philosophical or anatomical discussion.

Religions of all types have a harder time. Apart from the few religions that require their followers to be vegetarian or vegan, the majority of religions, and certainly the two major ones, rely on a book that they claim to be the word of God.
God surely must be constant and infallible and thus the teachings of whatever book they use must also be unchanging and infallible.
Yet these books tend to imply that man is a superior race from animals and thus has the right to eat and to sacrifice them without a second thought.

Now, it is never a good idea to start to question religious teachings and doctrines, because much of it makes little sense and, indeed, the followers of most religions are forbidden to question. They must accept these teachings as the infallible word of God.

Should a follower question his superiors about the correctness of eating animals, that DNA testing has demonstrated are largely the same as humans, he would, no doubt, get quoted at him chapter and verse, demonstrating that the saints of old ate meat and thus it is permitted to eat meat today.

Now, the problem is made more complicated, as we know that all is one and that one is the force we call God, despite each and every human or animal having a profound sense that they are individuals.

Further, we have stated that DNA applies exclusively to physicality and the non-physical aspects of man do not contain DNA and yet DNA must have auras, as everything has auras and auras are non-physical.

So, we have a great deal of unravelling to do before we can hope to understand DNA and its vital place in the construction of life.

So far, we have discovered that DNA exists and all creatures have it.
Apart from the fact that there is both DNA and RNA and the construction of this double helix we mentioned earlier is the result of the input of both the male and female bonding, we have not really discovered much.

Now, we mentioned that DNA - when we talk about DNA we also include RNA - is rather strange, in that it is of exceptional importance in the makeup of all life but only applies to physicality.

This is obviously not correct.

Usually, if anything exists in physicality it is because it exists in the non-physical aspects first.
DNA, as one can visualize and use in physicality, belongs exclusively to physicality but there is the non-physical counterpart that exists in a totally different form.
We will investigate this non-physical aspect later.

But, it is the physical aspect that we wish to reveal.
This is not going to be easy because science, in regard to DNA, has not really made much progress since its discovery.
It is generally used to identify samples of blood, tissue and, to a certain extent, vegetable matter, by comparing aspects of an unknown sample to aspects of a known sample, expecting to get a match.

This is all well and good but doesn't really assist science to investigate why DNA exists.

One would have thought that science would investigate how and why DNA exists by tracing its existence back down the line of life to try to discover its origin but, apparently not.

If it is true that DNA cannot exist in astral form, it begs the question that if, for example, an entity from the astral realms created a body that could appear in physicality, would that body have DNA?

And then we could go on to ask a further question, that to create a complete DNA profile we need input from, effectively, both male and female.
In normal people, this comes from the mother and father but if we take an example of a person who has completed his incarnation and who, obviously, had a mother and a father so, when incarnate he needed both DNA and RNA but, as we said, DNA effectively dies with the physical body.

Therefore, once the person returns home to the spirit world, he no longer needs, in non-physicality, DNA.

This is fair enough and not that hard to understand.

But, if we assume that this person develops the ability to create a secondary body to appear in physicality, where would the necessary DNA appear from?

We would like you fully to comprehend the complexity of this matter as it is important.

So, we will repeat the scenario.
1. A person is born and has a unique blend of genetics obtained from his parents. There is obviously more to this story but we will consider that later.
2. He has his incarnation and eventually dies. His body is disposed of and his DNA with it. His spirit rises to the heavenly spheres.
3. He decides that he wants to return to Earth for a short while to do a mission on Earth. We are not talking about reincarnation. We are talking about a guide who wishes to make a physical body for a few minutes or a few hours, to help someone incarnate.
4. So, from astral matter, he forms a body and lowers its frequency, until it can appear in the 6th dimension, which is your reality.
5. So, he appears to have a second body. One in non-physicality and the second one standing on Earth, as a solid person - as real looking as you are.

The question we asked was, where does the DNA come from to create this solid looking body?

We mentioned that for every object ever created, there was sufficient atoms of all sorts provided to allow a life to live in physicality, so we won't bore you with another detailed examination of that phenomenon.
Nor will we try to comply to strict scientific code concerning these microscopic aspects of life.
We are conveying information to the general public for their clarification and not writing scientific treaties.

This would be especially comical if science could really see the truth about atoms and the building blocks of life.
They would be profoundly shocked to realise that what they think that they know about atoms is only a tiny drop in the ocean in understanding the true nature of atoms.

What we have told you so far in our various publications was and is true but, it is only a tiny part of the reality. The rest will have to wait until humanity advances to the point where further revelations can be made.

Thus, let us return to the consideration of how an apparently fully-fledged, fully functioning human is constructed in physicality when required to render service here on Earth.

This would be quite complicated because, although the Directors of Life provided enough atoms for a person throughout his incarnation, once that incarnation is finished, those atoms are no longer required and logic would suggest that they would either disappear back to Prime Creator or, would be recycled in some way or another to avoid waste.

One thing would be certain and that is that the person concerned would no longer make use of atoms, as his one and only incarnation in physicality would be over - unless in some way sufficient, atoms could be stored somewhere, to provide that person with a reserve of atoms waiting in case the individual might choose to return to Earth for any reason.

A bit like having a wardrobe of clothes hidden away in case the person needed to don clothes again.
This also seems a bit unlikely. Can you imagine people in the spirit realms carrying a box or a bag about with them full of spare atoms, in case they became a guide and needed to use these atoms to create a new body for a while? The idea seems amusing but is not very practical.

But yet, we are aware that it is possible for an advanced guide to instantly create a human body to rescue someone from a tricky situation.

It may not happen very frequently but it does happen and that guide would create a body as alive as anyone else on Earth.
Thus, it would have DNA - or would it?

We will state, that in order to create a living copy in 3D of a person in the spirit realms, DNA is required.
In order to be alive, the created body must have all the attributes of a normal living person. Otherwise it would be a robot.

So, to cut a long story short, we will state that when a physical body is created;
a: The person needs a sort of blueprint upon which to fashion the body, and;
b: The person's Higher Self is able to fabricate all that it needs to clothe that blueprint.

This must sound very strange because, we are informed that in a normally born person, the DNA is a mixture of both parents DNA, which is passed down to the offspring.

This is one of the reasons that rich and influential people from all over the world go to great lengths to ensure that their children are actually the products of the mother and father that bear their name and that the mother does not have the opportunity to be impregnated from any outside source - at least until an "heir and a spare" are born.
Later offspring are less important.
What concerns royalty, etc., is that the royal line should be carried on in an uninterrupted fashion, as if the genes of the king had some special properties.

The fact that the genes of the king might contain faults, that might lead to madness, does not seem to concern them. Their arrogance is such that producing the next generation is all that matters.

Now, to a certain extent, it is true that aspects of the DNA are given to the children but DNA is far more complicated than that and, as DNA testing is still in its infancy, science looks no further than a few matching pairs between the parents and the offspring.

But, the most important is the so-called "junk" DNA, which actually contains the true aspects of the life force.
But, junk DNA is not an easy thing to quantify, because it appears dormant in a "living" person, as its activity is greatly connected to spirituality and also non-physicality.

So, in fact, there are two levels of DNA.
The first is the sort that science is aware of and that dies when the physical body dies.

The second is this so-called "junk" DNA, which is both physical and non-physical.

This junk DNA also has two aspects to it.

The first and most important is the spiritual or non-physical aspect, which is connected to the Higher Self and, indeed, the Akashic Record.

The second part is physical, in the sense that it is closely connected to physicality.

This is difficult to explain and so all that we can really do is to repeat what we have already said concerning DNA.

Ordinary DNA is a form of connection to the parents, although even ordinary DNA has aspects to it that have nothing to do with the parents but is related to the non-physical aspects of the person, that is to say, ID, Higher Self, etc.

However, junk DNA is a wonderful aspect of man.

It appears to lie dormant and for many whose souls still sleep, it does lie dormant but is closely connected to Higher Self and, even more, to the Akashic Record.

Obviously, we will talk about this at length later, as its effect on individual and collective life of man, past, present and, to a certain extent, future, is of the utmost importance.

We could question what form DNA takes in physicality?

Actually, there are not that many bits and pieces that go to makeup physicality and so DNA is a form of collective of atoms.
Most things are made of atoms combining in one form or another.
Atoms are virtually indestructible and as all atoms only exist to give meaning (form) to a living Logos, each and every atom is linked to something; animal, vegetable or mineral.

So, when a physical life form is finished with and its life energy withdraws, the atoms that were used to create that object and to help sustain its life are no longer required, they are freed from the task they were given, which was to sustain that object.
But we said that the items that made something live in physicality are no longer required but will never be used for anything else and, also, are virtually indestructible.
This seems to create a problem because, over time, as life forms come and go, so once something has left physicality, the countless atoms that made that something would remain in suspension, floating aimlessly for virtually all eternity.

This would seem an awful waste of energy and would clog up the world.
Thus, we can be sure that an answer was found.

Once something "dies"; animal, vegetable and, eventually, mineral and the atoms released, quite simply the Logos attached to each atom is removed and that atom now has no further use.
Therefore, the spiritual force of those atoms are absorbed back into the Godhead and, effectively, the atoms cease to be.

This is done slowly over a long period of time.

Thus it is, that something that is made of flesh and bone; human, animal; evidence remains for many years in the form of a skeleton and its DNA can still be traced, in some cases for hundreds or even thousands of years, depending on the conditions of preservation of the corpse.

But, eventually, all trace of that object disappears.

The atoms, now no longer required, are absorbed back into the force we call God.
Thus, is conservation of energy maintained in as efficient a manner as possible.

We need to be careful at this point, because we could easily get sidetracked into a discussion of the many and varied forms of atoms - some of which we have described and some which remained to be discussed at some point - but we are talking about DNA and so we really need to keep focused on that topic.
This is not easy as, not only is everything connected and is actually just different ways of describing oneness, but much of this oneness breaks down to a description of DNA.

What we are trying to describe to you is that so-called flesh, blood, tissue, skin, hair, bone, etc., does not, by chance, contain DNA.
These aspects of life are DNA and just happen to resemble flesh, blood, tissue, etc., that we mentioned just above.

We would like you to try to visualize that every aspect, every atom, every molecule of everything that exists is made, in all dimensions, from DNA.

Now, as you know, each person, each animal, each plant, not only has DNA markers that tell it and us just what it is in terms of human, animal, plant; not only tell us what species of animal it might be - lion, tiger, elephant, cat, dog or what type of plant it might be - rose, cabbage, carrot, etc.

It then goes on to tell us, and itself, its unique identity.

In the case of us humans, the DNA of each individual person could (and is) being mapped, in order to permit instant identification of the whole human race.
The same could be done, of course, for each animal, each plant and each piece of mineral.

If one wished, every single dog, cat, bird, lion, tiger, etc., could be mapped and the same done with every plant also.

To a certain extent, this is already done with farm animals in many countries.
Not using DNA but having each animal marked at birth with a unique number, that follows the poor creature up till the moment it is slaughtered and its body parts distributed for consumption.

If we pushed this idea onto its limit, try to imagine this!

If the DNA of any and all things was known and a huge database formed, it would be possible to take an unknown atom, analyse its DNA and compare it to something in the database.

Now, imagine we could make a sort of butterfly net, wave it about and capture one or more atoms floating in the air.

If we then analyzed one of these atoms for DNA, we would find that it would correspond to something in the database, thus demonstrating the veracity of our statements concerning the fact that each and every atom has a marker attached to it that tells the atom that it is designated to be part of a unique "something".

Of course, modern man has not yet managed to create such a database yet but existence has.
It is called DNA.
Can you imagine the outreach of that?

Through DNA, every aspect of everything has a marker that tells it that it is going to be a human or animal or plant or raindrop or stone.
Then, those items are grouped together to form an object; human, animal, etc.
Further, each and every atom has a marker that tells it which part of that entity it is going to be.

So, the DNA of everything is of overriding importance.

If we could take an atom at random, if we could sufficiently analyse its DNA, we could discover exactly what the designation of that atom was.

In the case of a human, if we captured an atom with our butterfly net and checked its DNA, we would know to which human that atom was destined and which part of the many body parts it was meant to help form.

All this is contained in the DNA.
Most of it is contained in the so-called "junk" DNA and so, we hope that you can appreciate just how remarkable DNA is and its importance in the construction of all life, in all dimensions.

And this is just the beginning.
DNA is an integral part of the Akashic Record, as we will explain later.

However, this chapter is meant to give you a brief overview of DNA as it applies to physicality and so we hope that we have been able to open your eyes to the fact that there is far more to DNA then comparing a blood sample to catch a criminal.

Having looked at DNA as regards physicality, we will go on to seeing what happens as we progress into the non-physical dimensions in other chapters.

CHAPTER 3

JUNK DNA – AN OVERVIEW

We have tried in the previous chapters to explain to you some of the physical attributes to basic DNA and have said that it remains with the physical form (body) of an object, whatever that object might be; human, animal, plant and, eventually, mineral and will decompose as the body decomposes.
So, we gave the impression that DNA is a purely physical part of life and, once that life is finished with, once the incarnation has terminated, DNA plays no further role.

In terms of basic DNA, the sort that was discovered in 1953 and that science uses today to classify things according to their DNA structure, it is true that it ceases to exist when whatever is being considered no longer has need of physicality. But we also mentioned 'junk' DNA.

Science, largely, ignored this sort of DNA because it did not seem to fit in with the first sort of DNA and, as unravelling the problems relating to basic DNA was difficult enough, it was considered prudent not to concern themselves with this other, strange form of DNA.

Perhaps this is just as well, as this so-called junk DNA is of such complexity, such importance, that we can almost be sure that any scientific study of it would have come up with incorrect interpretation and so, for once, we do not have to spend time in undoing incorrect concepts concerning it.
We have a blank slate to work with and so, in this chapter, we will give an overview of what junk DNA is.

First, let us say that we deplore the word junk in relation to DNA but as it is a term that most people are familiar with, we will continue to use that rather repugnant word, despite the fact that it is the complete opposite to any understanding that junk may have.

It is, as we have mentioned, of vital importance to all life, in all dimensions and life without this DNA could not be.

So, let us try to portray what this form of DNA is.

We mentioned that ordinary DNA contains sufficient information to enable scientists to identify most things.
First in the sense of human, animal, plant and mineral - although science has not yet developed the technique of isolating the DNA of minerals.
Then it is possible to identify each and every individual person, animal, plant and stone if science so desired although, of course, scientists stop at just identifying individual people but, through careful analysis of DNA, it could also be applied to individual animals, plants and minerals.

Now, the one question that is perhaps not asked is why?
Why should DNA be unique to every single object found on Earth?

This will take us into the rather complicated subject that we have mentioned before and that is that every atom, every particle that constitutes an atom, vibrates to a unique frequency.
You may remember us mentioning this previously.
But, although like all things it is simple, if one does not understand the concept, it can be difficult to explain and to comprehend.

The basic difficulty is that every atom has not only a unique vibration that sets it apart from any other atom but there are a number of sorts of atoms.

We have mentioned, for example, that every spot in the entire galaxy has a unique frequency and that frequency can be used by beings that have sufficiently sensitive measuring instruments to aid in navigating anywhere in the galaxy.

For those who do not understand what we are talking about, we will describe this again.

In all of the galaxy, there is no such thing as empty space. No such thing as a vacuum.
The entire galaxy - if we ignore for a moment individual people, animals, plants, stones and planets - in other words what we call "space", is actually crammed full of a special type of atom.

There is a reason for this but let us just say that nature abhors a vacuum and so nature has filled all of space with countless atoms.
These are not atoms known to man but, if they could be seen, space would be seen as a huge cloud of dots (atoms) each one of a slightly different vibration to any other.
Thus, it is that, if one knows the vibrational frequency of any spot, and if one causes one's spaceship to vibrate to that frequency, by the Law of Mutual Attraction, one would cease to be at one's point of departure and instantly appear at the point that corresponds to the particular vibration that one is now in harmony with.

This is a very useful method of travelling vast distances instantly.

But although this form of transport is somewhat known about, what is not known is that each and every spot can be considered to be a DNA point.

In other words, the entire galaxy is not only full of a special kind of atom - countless numbers of them - but each atom can be considered as part of the DNA of the galaxy.
But it is even more complicated than that.

Not only is each atom part of the DNA of the galaxy but each one of these atoms is, itself, a form of living object and thus has DNA.

So, each atom in the galaxy has this frequency that, if one can imagine it, has two purposes. It marks each spot in the galaxy and provides an aspect of DNA of the galaxy but, also, the item exists in its own right and thus has its individual DNA, which marks it uniquely from any other atom in the galaxy.

This vibration, although serving two purposes, uses the same one unique frequency.

We don't know if you can visualize this because, although it is not complicated, it is difficult to imagine.
So, let us try again using our butterfly net.

If we could go out into apparently empty space, wave our net about and capture an atom, we could examine that atom.

We had better repeat that science has no knowledge of these atoms that fill apparently empty space, but they exist.

So, we will take the atom that we have captured and, with a very sensitive frequency meter, measure the frequency to which it vibrates.
We will find that it vibrates to a certain frequency and, if we were able to capture a second atom and measure its frequency, we will notice that it vibrates to a different frequency.

Now, what we can't prove but ask you to accept, is that, that unique frequency, is what we call DNA.
DNA is vibration, although the way science measures it with their crude instruments does not suggest so.

The reason for that is that;
(a) The instruments are not sensitive enough to measure these frequencies and
(b) Science takes still photographs of DNA, in so any vibration would go unnoticed.

But to return to the atom of DNA in space, it plays a role in the DNA of the galaxy and also provides the DNA of that atom.
All this is because everything is alive and so everything must have DNA.

But never forget that Prime Creator - the entity that created the concept of everything - is itself pure light, vibration.
Light is a form of vibration.

So, everything that exists is vibrating. Vibration is the basis of life.

Further, this vibration is actually what we refer to as DNA.

As everything has a unique vibration, that unique vibration can be measured and we can say that no two things are alike.

It is this unique vibration that causes this and when we examine something and we noticed its uniqueness, we call that uniqueness DNA.

Can you visualize this?

Everything, everywhere in the entire multiverse, has a unique vibration, which is why it can be identified.
We call that uniqueness DNA.
So, everything is made of vibration and everything is made of DNA.

That is why DNA is so important.

Now, we are aware that when scientists measure DNA, they come up with a series of markers that they use to say that a sample of something does, or does not, resemble another sample but if they could actually measure the frequency of the sample they would see that it vibrates to a unique frequency and the markers are just stepping stones that enable them to identify something.
If they had instruments sensitive enough they would not need to plot these markers. They could just measure the frequency and see the similarity.

Obviously, from what we said, it would only be if the sample being measured was exactly the same as the reference sample, that the frequencies would be an identical match.

But there is another aspect to DNA, above and beyond the physical attributes of a sample.

All is one so all must have auras.

The auras will follow the life of an atom forever and so, once the physical part of the atom decomposes, the non-physical aspect continues endlessly on into and through the spiritual realms.

This is where junk DNA comes in.
There is a link between the physical and non-physical aspects of atoms and it is junk DNA that provides the link.

It can be considered rather to be the silver cord that links a physical object to its non-physical counterparts.
It is not quite like that but we do not have language to describe this link.

We mentioned it in the last book where we describe the attachment a young girl might have for her dolls. It is a form of love, of gravity but, as we said, we cannot use one word to describe this attachment. There is no word.

But nevertheless, the non-physical part of DNA follows the physical, and, eventually, the non-physical aspects of an atom for all time, giving a unique frequency to an atom no matter what dimension it might be in.

We hope this is not too confusing, because what we have described above in relation to an atom applies to all things, in all dimensions and for all time.

Nothing alters.
The reason is simple and we have mentioned it countless times.
All is one.
There is only one.

Now, you have, we hope, noticed that all things have the notion that they are separate, unique.
You feel strongly that you are a unique person, separate, not only from every other person but, even more so, from any animal, plant or mineral.

And yet we said that all is one!

So, what gives you this idea that you are separate from any other person or thing?
Quite simply it is DNA.
And even more so, junk DNA.

If all that existed was "non-junk" DNA, as that remains behind with the physical body, once we get to the non-physical realms we would all feel as one but this is not so.
For eons into the future we retain a feeling of being separate from any other person or creature and it is junk DNA that permits this.

The spiritual (non-physical) aspect of junk DNA stays with us when we "die" and remains with us in heaven.

The ultimate goal is to cast off that junk DNA and become one with all things - and with God - but that is a long way into the future for all of us.

So, we wish you to visualize clearly what DNA is and what junk DNA in particular is.

In simple terms, ordinary DNA is connected to physical objects and junk DNA is connected to the non-physical aspects of those same objects.

Obviously, this is an oversimplification of the truth of DNA but understanding the difference between the two sorts of DNA provides the first step in our comprehension of DNA.

We should, perhaps, go on and look at these two sorts of DNA and try to understand the difference that permits one sort to stay with the body and the other to stay with the non-physical aspects of something.

We have mentioned in other books the concept of markers, of flags and we mentioned that when breeding time for certain animals arrives, the cosmic clock triggers emotions to come forward that we referred to as the breeding cycle.

These emotions, we said, can be compared to an alarm clock that, once a pre-set moment arrives, the alarm rings.
We called that mechanism... flags.

This concept is used by nature frequently in a number of ways, for a number of purposes and in many dimensions.

To go back to DNA, we may say that these two types have markers, flags, attached to them that designate, not only their prime function, but also their other functions.

And there are many. We will do our best to describe the various functions as the book progresses.

So, what we wish to bring to your attention is the twofold nature of DNA, which is necessary to understand.

The first sort is the type that science uses, which is largely physical and the second sort is so-called junk DNA, which is both physical and non-physical.

It is this second type of DNA that is so important, as we will attempt to explain as we progress.

We cannot, at this point, indicate all the functions of junk DNA, as they are so many and are so intertwined with many, indeed most, of the other attributes that combine to create life, so all we can do at the moment is to give an overview of junk DNA and try to explain more in other chapters.

If and when a person dies, his physical body and his physical DNA - the first sort - dies, but his spirit and his junk DNA go with him into the spiritual realms and continues to do its job, one facet of which is to give a feeling of independence, of separatism from all other things, of the person.

So, could we describe junk DNA from a non-physical point of view?
We can try, although it is not going to be easy.

We have mentioned, in the past, Higher Self, Imagination, the ID and a number of attributes that all life has. We also mentioned the Akashic Record and have intimated that it is the personal record of the life of all things, uniquely recorded for all time.

It is this Akashic Record that may enable us to explain the role played by junk DNA, both in physicality and in the after life.

So, we hope that you will forgive us if we remind you of what the Akashic Record is and what it is not.

It has been called the Hall of Records and some people are under the impression that there is, somewhere underground, a vast hall, a library, full of recordings of some kind, complete with a librarian.
A moment's thought should demonstrate that this is nonsense and has been created by people of limited knowledge, who could not see any further than physicality.
Thus, as it is obvious that there is nowhere, either on the surface of planet Earth, nor in the skies where this huge library is housed, they imagined a hollowed-out area somewhere underground.
We should say that no one has seen this great underground hall, because it does not exist. But that does not seem to stop people from believing it exists.

Then there is a librarian.
Quite who this person is, his name, nationality and age are not mentioned.
As the Akashic Record has existed since man first existed, he should be approaching retirement age by now but, once again, people don't question who he/she is. They just accept that he is there doing his job.

If there were such a person, he would be quite a remarkable person; billions of years old, able to speak every language that has ever existed and able to keep track of countless trillions of recordings.
He would be constantly updating the library and constantly issuing files or recordings to those requesting information.

No one seems to mention from what these recordings are made, nor who is making them.

Is there a huge army of scribes, constantly recording every event throughout all the world and passing them to the librarian, or are there a huge number of video studios and every event is being recorded on to videotape and then passed to the poor overworked librarian?

You can see, we hope, just how ridiculous the whole story is but you would be surprised at the number of people who believe the Hall of Records myth.

However, the Akashic Record does exist and we have explained at some length that it is a non-physical (spiritual) concept that cannot really be seen because, although it does exist, it does not exist as a single building.
It is called The Living Library, which does not help much.

Even in the explanations that we have given concerning the Akashic Record, we skirted over some aspects of it at that time because one cannot hope to understand what the Akashic Record is until one understands what junk DNA is.

Both DNA and Akashic Record are connected and are, in fact, one and the same.

The Akashic Record is composed of the information of each and every person, animal, plant or mineral, because the Akashic Record is the information contained by DNA in general and junk DNA in particular.

We hope that you can start to see just how complex all of this is and how difficult it is, and will be, to explain in simple terms. But we will do our best.

Let us stay with the Akashic Record for a moment.
We have said that it can be compared to a giant filing cabinet and each and every person who has lived, is living or will live, has a drawer in that filing cabinet.

Before people rush off and say that the Great White Brotherhood have said that there exists somewhere a filing cabinet where records of everything are stored, let us make quite plain to you that we are speaking hypothetically.

There is no filing cabinet and there are no drawers containing people's records.

But, nevertheless, there is an area where all information is recorded.
Let us try to examine that place somewhat.

We will say, first of all, that it is in the 5th dimension.
All dimensions are multitasking and the 5th dimension is where DNA is linked to.

But, in fact, DNA is linked to the 5th dimension, because DNA and the Akashic Record are one and the same thing.
The 5th dimension was mentioned in the book we gave you about auras.

We also mentioned that the Higher Self, the life plan and a number of other things start in the 5th dimension but, we also said that much of what happens in the 5th dimension is also passed to the 6th dimension and, from many aspects, these two dimensions are linked and one could almost call them the same dimension.
However, let us stay within the 5th dimension, which is where the Higher Self comes from.
The problem is that Higher Self, we have said, there is only one of for all things over all time and yet each and every person or object has a sense of individuality.
It is DNA that gives this sense of individuality.

Thus, it is that, although there is only one Higher Self, everyone and everything thinks they are separate - physically and spiritually - from all other people or objects.

When one is incarnate, the first sort of DNA plays a role in creating the illusion that, from a physical point of view, all people (just to consider humans) are separate from each other and a blood or tissue sample can be measured to demonstrate this.
Then, once one passes into non-physicality, junk DNA maintains that illusion.
In fact, it is the other way around.

The junk DNA is constantly communicating out to the world the uniqueness of each person which is then passed to the first sort of DNA and a blood sample can demonstrate that uniqueness. But it starts with junk DNA.

So, in a running order, we have Higher Self (of which there is only one) and then each and every person has so called junk DNA which links to Higher Self and, effectively, divides the oneness of Higher Self into the individuality of a person or entity which, in turn, sends that information into the first sort of DNA while the person or object is in incarnation.

So, this sense of separateness enables each and every person or thing to have independent thought and actions and, each and every entity throughout time has created an endless series of snapshots and each of the snapshots are, in effect, recorded into the junk DNA of that entity and are stored for all time.
That record is what we call the Akashic Record.

This is all a bit complicated so we will explain it again.

In the way there are two things to consider.
The first is the Higher Self, of which there is only one for all things, whatever that thing might be.
Then there are what we call "things". This might be a human, an animal, a plant or whatever.
Now, these "things" do not actually exist as solid objects.
They are all creations of the God Force.
They are a concept, that have been given a sense of individuality by the Archangels that create existence.

Now, let us break off here for a moment and say that we will consider just humans, although what we will say will apply to all things.
But it will get a bit wearing to have to keep saying; humans, animals, plants, minerals and so on, so please understand that if we mention humans, we are referring to all life, in all dimensions, throughout all time.

So, in effect, us humans only exist as a sort of concept to which a Logos (the life force from God) was associated and that gives the impression that this human is a real being. In a way it is because the Logos is the seal from God to be alive.

But this is where it gets interesting.

If it all just stopped at that, then there would only be one person.
But, obviously, there are many more than just one person.
Looking back over time, through the present and into the future and then looking into the non-physical realms, there are an enormous number of people.

But, there is just one Higher Self, which is really what humans are. There is only one Higher Self so, in reality, there is only one person.
Don't forget, that when we talk about people, we are referring to everything.

So, to create more than one person, the concept of DNA was invented and placed with the Higher Self.

This implies that all things are really DNA, which creates the illusion of everything.
Can you understand this?
If it were not for DNA, nothing would really exist.

There is one God and his Archangels created one Higher Self, which is the representation of God. But there is only one Higher Self.
So, God, to give life to the cosmos, created this one Higher Self - or rather his Archangels did.

But this did not help God much in his quest for knowledge, so the Archangels came up with the concept we call DNA.
Obviously, this is light years away from the primitive idea of analyzing blood samples to solve crimes.

We are talking about a fundamental concept developed when existence was first created, that gave all life a sense of individuality.

We will say, that when early life was created, long ago in the 8th dimension, the other concepts; Imagination, Higher Self, etc., were also created, although the way that we had to explain it to you, chapter by chapter, gave the impression that things were created one at a time over vast amounts of time.
As time does not really exist, when life was first put into the 8th dimension, we can consider that Higher Self and DNA were also connected to early life.

This amazing DNA exists to this day and is what we call junk DNA.

We would like you to appreciate that all these various aspects to existence; Higher Self, Imagination, ID and so on are not actually separate elements of life.
They are all linked together and form a composite whole.

We have described them as independent facets of a living entity but, in fact, they are all linked and all pull together as if they were one.

This also is a rather difficult concept to fully appreciate, especially as we have stated that junk DNA exists in a very real form to give a feeling of independence, of uniqueness to everything, no matter what it might be.

It seems almost a contradiction to say that every part of a living object is linked together and yet junk DNA is doing all it can to make that living object feel that it is separate from any other object.

It seems an awful waste of energy for God's Archangels to have created every part of a living entity as linked and, at the same time, created DNA to create the feeling the complete opposite to that notion of being linked.

Let us, just as a mind exercise, imagine that if we had junk DNA so far developed that, not only would it make us feel separate from any other human (just to consider humans but we refer to all living entities) but also refuse to accept that it was in any way linked to Higher Self, Imagination and the many aspects that come together to create existence.

We have said that for many of these aspects of life there is only one of so, in this mind exercise, let us imagine that a person refused to accept that he shared these diverse elements of life with any other life form.

We know that this is unlikely but, in this mind exercise, let us imagine that the feeling of uniqueness created by DNA pushed the person to consider that he was the only one that really counted and that any other being or entity was not in any way connected to him.

Now, the question we might ask ourselves is, is it possible for someone to be so influenced by junk DNA, so as to consider himself as the only one that counts?

Unfortunately, the answer is yes.

There are a surprising number of people - and even animals and even more plants - that think exactly like that.

They are so influenced by this feeling of independence, of uniqueness, of self importance, that they consider themselves to be totally cut off from any form of consideration for any other life form.

Let us just consider humans.

These humans that are totally under the control of the DNA we call psychopaths.

It is considered that a psychopath is someone who cares only for his own wants, needs and desires and does all that is necessary to fulfill these emotions.
You can see that there have been throughout history and are, to this day, a large number of people who acted, and who act, in this manner.

Some have been known to history and some are unknown.

What is interesting is that it is DNA taken on to unbridled limits, that create what we call psychopaths.

It goes to show just what a powerful force DNA is and we have tried to demonstrate to you how very far reaching the effects of DNA are, especially of junk DNA.
Far outside of just comparing blood samples.

We will end this chapter here in which we gave an overview of junk DNA and move on to the next aspect which will consider DNA in a more cosmic sense.

CHAPTER 4

JUNK DNA EXPLAINED

So far, we have examined in fairly basic terms, what we might consider to be "standard" DNA - the sort that science examines.
We went on to examine what is called "junk DNA" and discovered some of its amazing properties with regard to the non-physical aspects of life and how very important that junk DNA is in creating and maintaining life in all dimensions, both physical and non-physical.
We cannot over emphasize the importance of DNA and we have said that it can be considered to be second only to the life spirit (the Logos of God) itself.

Now, we must go on to examine DNA with a somewhat more expanded vision and look into another area of life, about which very little is known to the general public but which, inevitably, leaks down through the chain of life into physical life itself which can be considered to be at the bottom of the well of life, if we can just imagine it.
We mean that, at the top we are in sunshine & light and as we descend down, it gets darker and darker until, in physicality, compared to the surface of the well, we are in murky gloom, wading about in the mud and slime of so-called reality.

We paint this rather dramatic picture to help you realize that life as you know it and as you experience it is all, actually, just aspects of spirituality and that none of it is real, although it does seem real.

It is all just a question of us being able to open ourselves to the light of God - or not!

For those who cannot, they seem to live in a horrible, bleak world, but for those who are able to allow the light of God into their hearts, life seems bright and pleasant.

Of course, as we have explained, the amount of light that may enter people's hearts is governed by the swing of the Cosmic Pendulum - as we have explained - that as we progress through ascension, so the upper edge of the well will be flooded with more and more light.
Therefore, people able to reach into that light will feel greater and greater levels of joy and, eventually, bliss.

However, the bottom of the well will remain always as dark and murky, so people will have a clear choice.

Either to progress towards the light or to remain at the bottom of the well.

It might seem crazy that anyone would wish to remain in darkness, with all the negative aspects that come with that; fear, hatred, jealousy and so on when, by allowing the light of God into their hearts, they could live in the light of God, with all the positive attributes that come with it.

However, there are a surprising number of people who prefer to remain in this gloom. They are people that we refer to as psychopaths, although there is a wide degree of consciousness between a true psychopath and those that are just depressed and lost.

The true psychopath is someone who thinks exclusively of his own needs and wants. But, we can be sure that if we question anyone who suffers from depression, to a greater or lesser degree, they will be feeling that life is treating them unfairly. Life is not supplying all that they think they require/deserve in order to feel happy.

No matter by what degree these needs and wants are satisfied, there is always another desire that remains to be satisfied.

With these people, nothing will persuade them to stop thinking of themselves and to devote their lives to helping others, which is the true secret of happiness.

In the degree that we can stop thinking of satisfying our own desires and turn to helping those less fortunate than oneself, by the Law of Mutual Attraction, we can fill our own lives with joy.

When we turn our backs on those that reach out to us for help, we are turning from the light and we are facing gloom.

Thus, it is that many people live in this gloom at the bottom of the well we described - and are "happy" to do so, if we can use a contradiction in terms.
Happy, implying being unhappy.

It is the refusal to change that is so sad.

We cannot help these people and it is pointless trying.

However, the good news is that consciousness marches on and the light of Ascension floods us with God's power a little more each day.

We can gradually see this and, if we look back just a few years, we can see a dramatic change in attitude.

More and more people are refusing to accept that a certain group could or should abuse children.
These people are being exposed more.
Some will be ejected from positions of power.
Others will be prosecuted or put in mental institutions.

Those that abuse animals are being exposed.

Those that create chaos through wars or by creating financial problems are being questioned.

In short, life is changing and a split is appearing.

The negative people who had such power a few years ago and who persuaded us that they had the right to live as they chose, are being abandoned by those feeling the influx of spiritual light.

At the moment we are in the infancy of Ascension but, as all life progresses from infancy to adulthood, so those who have chosen to follow the light will grow in numbers and in power and will overtake the evil or lost ones staying at the bottom of the well.

So, what will happen to those negative ones?
We have the right to remove them from positions where they can harm others but we do not have the right to harm them.

As those people come to the ends of their incarnations and are placed in hell to resolve their faults so, by the Law of Mutual Attraction, those choosing to incarnate will be more spiritually minded.
Thus, the population of Earth will gradually change from what it is now, to what it is destined to become.

Nothing can stop this progress.

Planet Earth will change into what it is destined to become - a Heaven on Earth, a Garden of Eden.

Now why did we mention all this?

This book is about DNA.

However, DNA is not a fixed material. It is spiritual in nature and so can be influenced by swings of the Cosmic Pendulum we mentioned.

Long years ago, when life was in the darkest grips of the swing of the pendulum of existence, the DNA of people incarnating was full of negativity and so it was considered normal for terrible deeds to be done and people flooded to places to watch, with great delight, some unfortunate person being tortured or executed.

It was considered normal for such events to be carried out in public and it was considered normal that huge crowds should gather to enjoy these scenes.

Of course, this is still being carried on in certain Eastern countries.

It is still going on in some countries in Europe where people attend bullfighting.

It also still occurs where the public turn up to watch others chase over the countryside to watch a fox hunt or to watch others slaughtering beautiful birds; partridges or pheasants.

Big game hunting is still going on and photos of magnificent animals, killed by some rich few, are displayed on social media.

To a lesser degree, the modern-day equivalent of Roman arenas goes on.
We call it football or rugby, but it is based on gladiatorial fights conducted in a Roman arena.

So, we are not out of the woods yet but awareness is changing and we have less and less people approving of the barbarous acts of killing wild creatures and more people protesting and taking action to stop these practices.

Eventually, of course, all these primitive actions will stop as we progress to the point that those who are rising in Ascension will be in a position to pass laws banning all primitive actions by those left at the bottom of the well.

All this happens as DNA alters.

We repeat, DNA is not just a fixed form that denotes the blood type of a person. It is a living object in its own right, closely connected to spirituality and can change as people ascend - or not.

It goes much further than that.

When a person's incarnation comes to an end and he/she "dies", the spirit of that person goes to the upper fourth dimension that we call Heaven.
This dimension, like all the dimensions, is cut into many, many layers, depending on the level of spirituality of the people who inhabit those areas.

We will repeat, once again, that hell is part of the upper fourth dimension and is, itself, multi-layered.
It is not in the lower fourth dimension, nor is it at all as described in religious texts.

Hell responds to people's states of spirituality.

So, from what we might refer to as the default area, "Summerland", it descends down, just like going down the well we mentioned earlier until, at the lowest level, it is horrible indeed and the only area below that is one where the person chooses to give up the life spirit all together.
This, fortunately, is extremely rare and most people cling to life no matter how dismal it is.

Who are these people that inhabit those areas?

They are people that had an incarnation long ago when life was in its darkest part of the Pendulum swing and who delighted in causing as much pain and unhappiness as possible, to as many as possible.

They considered that they had the right to do this, showed no remorse when they had their life review and so went to the stygian depths, which is where they were and are spiritually.

However, even today it is not uncommon for certain people to be at a similar level and hell contains a number of powerful people; kings, queens, princes, dictators, politicians and religious leaders who lived a life of debauchery and considered that they had the right so to do.

Heaven does not judge.

The Law of Mutual Attraction comes into play.
People have a life review, which gives them the chance to show remorse for any harm they have caused.

Those that feel fully justified to live as they lived, being cut off from any sentiment of connection to others, are drawn to a level of hell corresponding to their attitude with regard to all life.

Conversely, others who devoted their lives to helping others as much as they could, are drawn to a sunny part of heaven.

Those we consider ordinary people are drawn to Summerland.

The strange thing is that all this is connected to DNA and, specifically, junk DNA.

How is this possible?

We have suggested to you that DNA is what causes us to think that we are individuals, cut off from any other life form which, at its extreme end gives us Psychopaths, but there is another, completely opposite aspect to DNA.

This is also going to be a bit difficult to explain.

We have stated that all life is one and that one is God.

But, at the same time, DNA gives us the feeling of being separate.

However, just as each atom of everything has both auras and DNA - which is the way all living things are constructed - so DNA, which is alive, also has auras.

This may not be easy to visualize.

Inside every atom of everything is DNA and that DNA, being alive, is connected to all life and thus has auras as all life has.

The implication of this is that DNA can be influenced by its auras.

The big question is, of course, what could possibly affect DNA, as it seems a fixed quantity with living things?

We could go on and ask what would be the effect of modifying DNA?

So, we will open Pandora's Box again and see what flies out.

There is an aspect of auras that is outside of anything we have so far discussed.

Up until this moment we have done our best, in the various books and publications we have given you, to describe the eight dimensions, or auras as they are called, and have explained the countless sub-dimensions within these dimensions.

We have also examined alternative realities and time travel and a number of other things.

We have discussed the kindergarten where life is made and we could argue that there can't be much more to life to explain.

We must say that life is endless and, no matter how much we explain, we will never get to the end of the mysteries of life. It is truly monumental and staggering in depth.

So, without apologizing, we will introduce you to a new aspect that is not generally known.

There is an area of existence, where there is only what we can describe as a sort of giant mill.
Now, a mill is designed to crush seeds and things to transform them so that, in the case of wheat, the indigestible seeds can be turned into flour from which bread is made.

One could scarcely imagine aspects of life being ground up and transformed into something else, but this is exactly what happens.

What aspects of life would be chosen to be ground?
Why is it necessary and what would be the result?

Let us say straight away that we are talking figuratively.
There is no giant mill grinding things up but there is a place in existence where life forms - particular lifeforms - are changed, modified.

This can happen because some aspects of life are like grains of wheat. They exist, are created by the God Force, but are not "digestible" in the form that they are so they need to be modified so that they can be used by life.

What are we talking about?

Information which comes from the Higher Self is one example.
Information is given in blocks, which the human is not able to process directly and so it is necessary for a block of information to be modified into a stream of information which can, itself, be divided up into small packets of information which Imagination can accept, understand - or not - and can be passed on to the ID, etc., or rejected if it is not acceptable to a person.

Therefore, there is need of a mechanism which can take a block of information, transform it into a stream and pass it onto the next stage.

This mechanism is junk DNA, or rather an aspect of junk DNA.

The way this works is as follows.

We have told you that the Higher Self and junk DNA is contained in the 5th dimension which, itself, has a link to the 6th dimension which is where Imagination is contained.

So, when a person wishes to know something, a request is sent to the Higher Self and that Higher Self, if it considers that the person is ready to receive an answer, sends a block answer out.

There are some people who are able, in special circumstances, to receive blocks of knowledge.
When this happens, the person concerned puzzles about a problem and, all of a sudden, the answer, complete, appears in the mind of the person.

This obviously is very useful and is a way that many will be able to think in the future. At the moment it is quite rare and only a few, gifted people, are able to handle blocks of information.

Most of us need the information broken down into a series of short streams of information which they mull over before being able to accept another short stream of information.

Therefore, it takes the average person quite a while to receive a complete answer to a question, an answer that someone, able to receive and understand a block of information, would understand in a microsecond.

But, to go back to the average person.

Once the Higher Self has issued a block of information on any subject, it is passed to the next stage which is junk DNA.

This so-called junk DNA is multitasking, as are virtually all aspects of life, and there is an area of DNA that can take information from the Higher Self and unravel it into a long, logical stream.

DNA is able to think for itself and so it is constantly active, processing different aspects of life, very much like a sort of brain in its own right.

It is a truly amazing aspect of life - all life - and works in many areas doing many things, most of which are passed on to various parts that go to make up a living object.

The part of DNA that we are considering here is able to take a block of information and, according to the degree of intelligence of the person with whom it is attached, according to the previous knowledge that the person might have on the subject being requested, unravels the information and sends it to the Imagination in longer or shorter files of information.

We do realize that we have not really explained how DNA unravels this information but we cannot, in any logical fashion, explain how all this is achieved.

So, we must ask you to accept that, within so called junk DNA, there is an area which devotes itself to the task of making blocks of information digestible.

It does more than just this.

Transforming blocks of information from the Higher Self into streams digestible by Imagination is only one of its functions.

Another one is connected to the way auric power is accepted into the body.

We mentioned in another book that auras are constantly pouring energy into the body via the etheric double.

We did mention that this energy comes in different powers and it was the job of the etheric double to balance this power to try to make all the aspects of a living entity to be in balance.
This force that balances the energy is DNA which works in harmony with the etheric double and, in effect, tells the etheric double to allow more power through or to reduce the power entering the body.

So, the etheric double contains the valves that open and close at the various chakra points but the brain that controls the etheric double chakra points is junk DNA.

Let us explain this again in slightly more detail.

The human body is able to operate as it does, partly, due to the auras of which there are eight.

Auras and dimensions are the same thing but it seems better to talk of dimensions when we are referring to the rather complicated aspects of existence and refer to auras when we are considering just the aspects of life in which power is poured into the body, keeping it alive and keeping the various parts of personality functioning.

Now, as we have said, each one of these auras is connected, at one end, to a personality aspect and at the other end to a part of the body which is designed to accept these personality aspects.

So, there are eight auras surrounding the body and, to enable the energy to enter the body, we have what are called chakras which are, quite simply, entry points for the auric energy to enter the body. All things have eight chakras.

But this auric power may be too powerful to enter the body directly, so a series of valves are placed between the auras and the chakras to regulate his forces.

These valves are placed in the etheric double.

But these valves must have some intelligent force telling the valves to open and close and it is an aspect of junk DNA that is this intelligent force.

This junk DNA can think for itself and can decide to open or to close any valve, thus regulating and balancing the auric power flowing into the body.

However, junk DNA can itself be influenced by the personality bundles flowing through the auras and into the body.

A human, for instance, has a personality which is outside of the personality bundles that operate in and on the body.

We are getting into deep waters here, but it is important that the amount of auric energy containing any one aspect of personality, that the DNA strives to balance, so that the person acts in an harmonious manner, can be modified according to the desire of the person, be understood.

We will explain this again.

In an ideal person, the personality bundles flowing through the auras and into the body via the chakras which are controlled by DNA, would all be balanced and the person would be a nice, kind, gentle, loving person.

But, people also have personalities apart from the personality bundles that are in the various dimensions or auras.

Although we have mentioned this before, we have not really discussed this personal aspect of personality, although we will at some stage. If not in this book, we will in another.

Anyway, let us assume that the person has an overdeveloped sex drive or an overdeveloped sense of self importance.
In that case, this driving personality aspect can influence DNA and can tell it to let more power into one of the chakra points connected to that aura and the DNA allows more of that aspect in and we see the person with an overdeveloped sex drive or an overdeveloped sense of self importance.

So, getting off the subject of DNA for a moment, we introduce you to the fact that we have the personality bundles that we have talked about but there is also another aspect to personality that is outside of and remote from the personality bundles and is under the control of the ID, and we will speak about that another time when we are dealing with other aspects of existence.

So, let us return to DNA.

We hope that you have understood that one of the many roles of DNA is to act as a sort of filter between the auras and the energies that flow into a human and helps to control the way the etheric double balances the energies in an attempt to create a balanced person.

We link this to the mill concept because, once again, the energy flowing into a person from the auras does so in a sort of flood of information - auric information - and the body would have the greatest difficulty in assimilating this auric power, almost as if a high-powered fire hose was to blast someone with water. It would damage the person but, thanks to DNA, this blast of energy can be modified, lessened until it becomes acceptable to a person, animal, plant or mineral.

We could go on but we hope that you have understood that this junk DNA plays a vital role in aiding life to live according to the power of that life form and according to the degree of spiritual energy that the life form contains.

We hope that you can realize that no two people are the same.

Some people, for instance, are barely human in spiritual terms and some are extremely advanced spiritually. We are including those no longer in incarnation in this assessment.

Therefore, we hope that you can realize that, in the first case, the DNA would have to keep the valves almost closed to avoid overloading the person with spiritual power, power that the person could not handle.
In the second case, the opposite obtains.

An advanced being would be able to absorb much more power then an undeveloped person and thus the DNA can open the valves much more and allow a huge amount of spiritual, auric energy, into the person.

Then, of course, we have a large number of people in between these two extremes, each person having his DNA allowing more or less auric power into the person's body.

Thus, we hope that you can see that the DNA of any two people is not quite the same and thus no two people are the same.
This applies to all things; animal, vegetable and mineral.

We may consider two flowers, for example, and they may seem identical to our eyes, but if they could be seen with the auric senses, they will be seen to be unique, separate products of their species. They would not be clones.

This sense of individuality is very important in development and it is the junk DNA, which is slightly different for all things, that helps create the impression of separatism.

There is more to this story than just DNA, but if it were not for DNA being alive and being part of every living object, they would tend to be clones of each other.

After all, there is one God, one Identity (ID), one Imagination, one Higher Self so, logically, all things should appear to be identical to each other.

But it is, in part, thanks to junk DNA, that all things are aware that they are separate, unique aspects of whatever they are; human, animal, plant or mineral.

We have given a fairly expansive explanation of so-called junk DNA although, as we so often have to say, we have only scratched the surface.

DNA and, especially, junk DNA, is of the utmost importance in the development of life but covers so many aspects of life that it would be quite impossible to fully explain all the attributes that DNA have.

As we progress through this book, we will discuss other aspects of DNA as far as we feel that you can understand but we must say that, like many aspects of life, DNA is so complicated that it would be beyond the comprehension of even the wisest of you if we really delved into a complete description of DNA, but we will explain as much as we can.

CHAPTER 5

DNA & THE RIVER OF LIFE

Having discussed DNA and its effects in physicality and having explained a certain amount about so-called junk DNA which, as we have tried to convey to you, is of paramount importance to all life, whatever form it takes, we will now move on to discuss another aspect, which is the way that DNA can affect the personality aspects of existence and we will look at it from the point of view of how humans are affected by DNA.

We did discuss the personality bundles of human life in the book about aliens, but we did not discuss how and why a personality bundle decides to do whatever it does.

By that we mean that a personality bundle might decide to remain with the person to whom it is attached or it might decide to wander off and act independently from the person and explore other aspects of life, as if it had an independent life of its own and is not just a reflection of the person that it is part of.

This power to act independently is due to DNA - junk DNA.

As we will be talking exclusively about junk DNA, we will stop using that rather derogatory term and just call it DNA.

Now, this DNA is complex and marvelous beyond our ability to imagine and is a wonderful aspect of life in virtually all domains.

It is rare that we can examine any aspect of life that is not affected, to some degree, by DNA.

It is strange that mankind ignores DNA, apart from comparing samples of blood or tissue, because the astral versions of DNA are involved with virtually every aspect of life, no matter which part we might investigate and which aspect of life we wish to examine.
At some point we always come across DNA aiding, modifying and guiding life.

Now, we must not confuse DNA with the angelic forces, nor should we give it attributes that it has not got.

DNA is not the life force, nor is it actually alive in the sense that you are, but so powerful and all-encompassing is DNA, that we could almost consider it to be alive.

DNA is not alive in that sense, but so intelligent is DNA that it resembles life closely and operates in the physical and astral bodies of humans - and all other life forms - constantly and in many areas.
So, we will try to explain how DNA can affect the personality bundles of a human as they go through existence in association with a human.

Now, we explained as clearly as we could the personality bundles of a human and explained that they could choose to remain closely attached to a human or could detach themselves and explore other avenues.

In order to make these choices, some form of intelligence, independent from the human concerned, needs to operate, providing the consciousness that enables personality bundles to make decisions.

On their own, they are just aspects of a person and have no independent ability to act on their own, but thanks to DNA they can be guided and directed to act outside of their prime directive, which is to help a human through his incarnation.

So, we hope that you have read and digested the book about aliens, book five, because we do not want to describe them all again.

But we will expand slightly on these personality bundles and how and why they are formed, helping and guiding a human through his incarnation and for long afterwards in the astral realms.

For a person to be truly alive, obviously, he needs to have a personality and so, long before he becomes a true living human, he is helped by guides and angelic forces to choose which sort of person he wishes to become.

At his conception, he is just a point of life and, at random, when a human is required to be created, an Archangel dips into the bank of life and selects, at random, a point of life and puts the Logos with it that tells that point of life that it is going to be a human.

From there, a number of important decisions are taken to allow this point of life to grow as a human, as opposed to a raindrop, an animal or a grain of sand.

It is considered that humans are at the top of all creation although, when one considers how some people act, it is not always obvious!

But the potential of humans far outstrips even the most intelligent of animals so, in theory, we can say that humans are at the top of life.

So, humans are gradually formed and each one is nurtured and cared for by angels who groom a life spirit to understand what is expected of a human.

Thus, each human is introduced to the personality aspects that all humans have access to.

This is a vast gamut of subjects.
The embryo human is introduced to all that we know of about personality from the lowest, cruelest, to the most noble, loving aspects of personality.

This next bit is going to be difficult to describe but, basically, as the young human spirit is introduced to all these aspects, so he feels drawn to some of them more than others.

This is because the young spirit already has DNA attached to him and, although this DNA is also young and without experience, it can draw on the experiences of previous generations of DNA and can associate more with some aspects of personality than with others.

We will expand on this subject as it is very complicated to understand.

The first thing we need to understand is that there are two time zones, if we may describe them as such.

A young human in the astral realms may well be a new arrival but the Higher Self, ID, Imagination and DNA have been around since the dawns of time in the eighth plane, which was a vast time ago.
Thus it - the young human - has access, or rather is influenced, by two types of information.

One part is the knowledge concerning humanity as it applies exclusively to this new person and the second part is the vast amount of information that all life has experienced by sharing the one Higher Self, ID, Imagination, Curiosity and DNA, which has been around since the beginning.

Therefore, we have this young human who is introduced to virtually every aspect of personality in existence and who needs, eventually, to make a decision as to which aspects he wishes to adopt.

We have a similar set up as a young person progresses through the educational system.
He will be asked, if he wishes to go to university, for example, which series of courses he feels drawn to.
This might include mathematics, art, sport or any number of educational paths.
Of course, a student will pursue a number of subjects, either closely or distantly related to his chosen path.

It is very similar with a young human in the astral realms.
He will be shown a large gamut of subjects (of personality attributes) and his tutors will take note of those he seems drawn towards.

For those who did not have the advantage of having a classical education, we wish to say that when we refer to "he", we are also referring to females (she).
We are aware that it is the custom in some countries to refer, systemically, both to he and she when writing or speaking in order to be gender correct, but please accept that it was considered normal in classical education to refer just to the masculine, it being accepted by all that is also included the feminine.

It in no way is meant to be derogatory to females. It is just used to lessen the number of words used to describe any attribute.

Perhaps those who wish to be gender correct could come up with a new word to describe he/she without needing to write the two words each time.

After all, it was done with the words miss and misses in order not to distinguish between an unmarried or a married female and the word Ms. was invented.

But, until a genetic term for he and she is thought of, we will continue just to say he and hope that ladies can accept that we include them also. Life is not sexist.

But to continue.

We have a young person who is introduced to all aspects of personality and note made of those to which he feels naturally drawn.

At that point, DNA starts to take an active role in developing these aspects of personality.

As we have said, DNA can think and act almost as if it is alive - although it is alive as all things are alive - but we mean that it can act almost as an independent personality.
DNA is very curious and is very complicated.

So, DNA starts to interact with a person's interests and begins to help form and encourage those interests, so that they become part of the makeup of a person.

These interests we refer to as personality bundles.

Now, this is where it gets quite complicated because, although DNA helps to form the personality bundles, it does not stay as part of the personality bundles.

Once it has done its job of helping form the character of a person, complete with all its personality aspects, it withdraws from that task and looks for something else to do.

Naturally, what we have explained above is not exactly how DNA interacts with personality and we have presented a simplified version of reality. Nevertheless, what we have described is close enough to reality that you may accept this as true.

Those of you who have read our other books where we mentioned that a person, when he is created, travels along one of the twelve paths that are known as the signs of the Zodiac - Taurus, Gemini, Pisces, etc - may be wondering how all this interacts with a person's personality bundles.

This is another area where DNA plays an active role.
Once a person has chosen his personality bundles, this obviously colours his outlook on life and, although he is still in the astral realms and is quite an unsophisticated person at that time, his personality is sufficiently formed so as to give him a distinct outlook on life and thus is ready to decide on which path of the signs of the Zodiac he wishes to progress.

Once again, DNA takes charge of the person and, in effect, helps the person make the decision as to which aspect of the Zodiac signs he wishes to follow.

We might consider DNA to be a sort of guide, a counsellor, who understands which one of the twelve paths would be the most suitable and thus guide the person to accept the influence of the chosen path.
In fact, each one of these paths exist because of DNA.

We will explain this, although it is very complicated.

We need first to say that, in the astral realms energy is never wasted so, although for each person who is alive, has lived or will live, he may choose which one of the twelve paths to follow, once the decision is made, in effect, the other eleven possible paths are no longer needed and so they disappear.

In fact, all of these twelve possible paths that are referred to as the signs of the Zodiac are actually created by DNA and as DNA is guiding the person towards just one of the paths, it is only necessary for one path to be created.

The other eleven paths are not created because there is no need of them. But should a mistake be made and it is realised that a person is not on the correct path, a new path - another aspect of the signs of the Zodiac - will be created and the person moved to this new path, in which case the previous path disappears.
It is all made of astral energy which is under the control of will, desire, and so can be created or made to no longer be by acts of will and it is DNA that has the power to create or uncreate these paths.

Once again, we will say that it is all a lot more complex than we have explained but what we have told you is true.
We have quite simply left out all the complications caused by Higher Self, the individual life plan of the person and many other factors which could make comprehension almost impossible.

In later books, as what we are telling you now becomes accepted into universal consciousness, we will be able to explain more, but for the moment, please try to accept that we present a basic overview of life and have to leave out the fine details, which would not help at all in understanding.

One advanced aspect we will mention concerning these parts of the Zodiac is one that was talked about in a video.
It concerns an advanced person being able to accept more than one sign of the Zodiac into his personality.

This would be very difficult to do, as you might appreciate, if you have understood what we have mentioned above.

Let us recapitulate.

We said that, with the aid of DNA - and other aspects that we did not mention - a person is given a personality bundle.
Then we said that DNA creates the most suitable path (sign of the Zodiac) for that person.

Don't forget that all this is created seven more times as well, implying that all these personality paths are created eight times in eight different dimensions.

Now, we are saying that a person can also create a modified version of his personality bundle and a new path - sign of the Zodiac - can be created and all of it introduced into a person alongside his first set of personality aspects.
Then all this is created eight times as well.

Then it was suggested that this could be done with all twelve signs of the Zodiac, in which case a gestalt occurs and the person is transformed into a sort of super being.

Now, we will say that this is possible but is so rare as to be not worthy of our consideration.

You will agree, we think, that we all have enough problems just dealing with the vagaries of one personality bundle and path without trying to develop more than one.

But what we are considering here is how DNA interacts with all this personality.

We will just repeat the main points.
1. The person is introduced to all the possible personality aspects available and note taken of any that the person feels naturally drawn towards.
2. DNA guides the person to accept his personality aspects into his personality bundle, which is repeated seven more times.
3. Then, DNA creates what we call the sign of the Zodiac, which corresponds to that person and places the person on that path, which will help and guide him for long years into the future, both physical and non-physical.

It is DNA that is controlling and, to a certain extent, creating all this personality stuff.

We have also mentioned that not all people choose to incarnate on Earth, but for those that do, a further stage is introduced.

We have said in a previous book that there are, placed in the etheric realms, twelve planets, each one corresponding to an aspect of the twelve signs of the Zodiac and a person destined to incarnate spends a certain time there until the planet Earth turns and aligns itself to a certain sign, at which point the person waiting to incarnate makes the leap from that Zodiac planet and associates itself with the chosen baby about to be born and we say that the baby is born under the sign of Aquarius, Pisces, Leo, Sagittarius or whatever and thus will have a certain personality.

Whilst this is true and is fairly automatic, we must also mention that DNA is also present and is keeping a watchful eye on proceedings, because the person incarnate will be using DNA for all his incarnation, and for long after, so DNA is present, pushing and guiding events to unroll as was planned, because all this process - from creation as a spirit point and into incarnation - is so complicated, that there is always room for error and DNA, in conjunction with guides and angels, needs at all times to monitor the situation and to deal with problems as they arrive.

Therefore, we wish to go back in time and describe, perhaps in other words, this very complicated procedure that creates for you the life you lead and the destiny you are drawn towards.

We do this because we have described the signs of the Zodiac in rather a piecemeal fashion and we feel that some of you might be rather concerned and have not understood how all this joins together, very much like a small stream flowing until it joins other streams, which become a mighty river, which joins other rivers and, eventually, forms a sea.

This analogy is so apt that we asked you to retain it in your mind and compare it to the information - the explanation - that we are about to give you.

So, let us go back to the point where you were little more than a point of life, created into a human by having the Logos of God given to you which was, and is, the stamp that tells you that you are a human and will remain a human until the end of time.
We just remind you that it is by pure chance that you were given the human stamp.
You could have been made into anything at all: a raindrop, a virus, a beast of some kind, a stone - anything!
But, by pure chance, as a human was needed, you were plucked from the mass of life spirits and giving a human stamp.

This should tell you that it was pure luck, pure chance that the Archangels selected you as a point of life to become a human.
So please, never think that you are superior to anything else. You are not.
It was just luck that you were selected.

However, having been selected gives you a certain responsibility above any other of God's creation.
Not superiority, but responsibility, to care for yourself and for all of creation.

Now, it was decided that life was too complex for an ordinary person to have all the aspects of personality because, being a human entails having a personality.

This, actually, is a two-part creation.

The first is to have a general aspect of one of the signs of the Zodiac and the second is to have your personal aspects within that sign.
Each person is different because of these personality aspects.

But, from the point of view of this particular discussion, we wish you to realise that, at one point, you did not have a personality, just being a point of life plus Higher Self, ID, Imagination, Curiosity, etc.

So, your tutors introduced you to all the different aspects of possible personalities and note was made of which one you felt most attracted to.
This is part of the Law of Mutual Attraction.

As curiosity is part of the fundamental aspects of humanity, your curiosity drew you to be more interested in one particular aspect of the twelve possible personality trends that we referred to as the signs of the Zodiac.

As we have said, this can be compared to school, where your teachers noted that you were more interested in certain subjects than others and thus placed you in a stream that developed those subjects.

Or, we could imagine twelve roads or twelve railroad tracks and you are placed in a vehicle on a road or railroad track.

Or yet again, we could imagine a small stream and you are placed on that stream to float down it.

However we imagine it, it is important to realize that this path, this sign of the Zodiac, will remain with you for all eternity, no matter what happens until, one day, far into the future, you can join the great sea of advanced humans, who relinquish their individual personalities, add it to the mass of other people's personalities and accumulated knowledge, and join with this great sea.
Rather as if you had been a drop of water in a stream and had flowed ever onward, endlessly towards a great sea, at which point the drop of water loses its individual personality and becomes part of the ocean.

This ocean of people giving up their individual personalities and joining a huge group of similar people, we refer to as God.

This magnificent, imaginary ocean we described is your destiny and it is to return to the God Force, from whence you came as a point of life.

But, it is thanks to the personality you had - and now have - that you experienced so much, learnt so much and became so wise that enables you, eventually, to arrive at your destination and join with all the other similar people and become part of the God Force.

We wish to repeat this, briefly, again.
You, in conjunction with your tutors (guides, angels and DNA), chose a particular personality path and you will walk that personality path for all eternity.
This path we call one of the signs of the Zodiac: Pisces, Aries, Gemini, etc. One of the twelve main aspects of personality.

We cannot over stress the importance of DNA in this long journey.

Your tutors tend to remain in the background, gently prodding you along, allowing you to try your strengths, making mistakes and learning by burning your fingers, so to speak, in the school of hard knocks, but DNA plays a much more active role.

We mentioned some time ago that life is being continuously created, destroyed and recreated billions of times a second and, in the gap where nothing exists, DNA is slightly changed for all things to help keep life in balance, in a creation where nothing is static and your DNA is what slightly changes you, billions of times a second to help keep you progressing down the river of life, as it flows ever onwards.

This will be the subject of the next chapter.

CHAPTER 6

DNA & THE BUBBLE OF LIFE

The way that life is created, we have already mentioned in previous works.
We have stated that existence is created and destroyed billions of times a second and that during the brief moment when life no longer exists, the Archangels, charged by God to create and control life, alter the DNA of everything, to keep existence in line with the ever-changing progress of what you refer to as time.

We hope that you understand to what we refer, which is why we have encouraged you to read carefully the books we give you, so that we don't have to keep repeating ourselves, which is time wasting for us and, no doubt, frustrating for those that have studied all the books.

So, we will progress with this chapter and ask those who do not understand, to do their homework.

It will be obvious, we hope, for you to understand that, during the moment where nothing exists, not everything is annihilated.

If this were to happen, life would just stop, so there must be some force still in existence that monitors all life, effects change where necessary and brings life back to reality again.

We don't know if you can appreciate just how extraordinary this event is?

Ever since life was created, countless millions of years ago, a snapshot of every detail of the entire galaxy was taken (formed if you like) and recorded for all time in the Akashic Record and then the film rolled onto the next frame, but during the moment the film was rolling onto the next frame, everything was slightly altered both in time, movement and DNA and then another snapshot taken.

And this is happening billions of times a second and has been occurring since the dawns of time and will continue endlessly into the future.

It sounds preposterous we agree.
Who came up with the idea?
Why is it necessary?
Where can all these countless still images be stored?
What sort of filing system is in place to allow someone to locate a specific event amongst all this mass of events?
Could not a simpler system have been invented?

One thing is certain. If we have such a complicated system in place, we can be sure that it is necessary.

The Archangels who created all this are not ignorant and we can be sure that they examined every possibility before creating existence as it is.

So, there is little point in arguing the pros and cons of why the system is as it is. We must accept life as we find it and do our best to comprehend.

We will also say that, so far, although we have examined a number of aspects of life and have revealed to you some areas that were previously unknown, we have just scratched the surface of the subject.
There are areas of life so advanced, so far beyond comprehension, that we doubt that we will ever be able to get to the point where we will say that there is no more to be said. If ever we get to that point, you will be able to understand why creation seems so complicated.
But, it is a fascinating journey for those interested in existence and for those able to comprehend.

Unfortunately, there will be many who are either not that interested or who find that they cannot understand and will drop out as the journey progresses.

Then, of course, we have the unfortunate souls who are so wrapped up in either religion, science or previous collective consciousness and think that what we reveal to you is so different from what they think is truth (from previous information given to them), that they reject what we tell them.

We appreciate the dilemma of those people and wish we had means of resolving their difficulties but, unfortunately, religion and science, often created by people lacking knowledge or for reasons not with the best interests of humanity at heart, have so muddied the waters of truth, as to put a psychological barrier between what is currently considered knowledge of life and the actual truth.

We go to great pains to present to you the wisdom that has been garnered together by people dating back many thousands of years and, in spirit form, are still studying esoteric and physical aspects of existence and have presented that knowledge to us to help educate you.

Our duty is to give you this knowledge, which will become apparent as the Ascension process advances. Knowledge of existence is part and parcel of Ascension.
You cannot rise in spirituality if you are ignorant of how life is constructed which, if you think about it for a moment, gives us a clue as to why the blocking or creating of false information has been the norm until now.

It gives us no pleasure to say that those who refuse to learn in this university of life will find it very difficult, if not impossible to advance spiritually.
The two go hand in glove together.

The strange thing, is that most people are able to accept that the master Jesus was not only a master of spirituality, but also had a great deal of knowledge of the mysteries of life and yet, many of those people accept the teachings of Jesus but refuse to learn, themselves, of these mysteries.

They do not realize that the master Jesus was who he was because of a mastery of both spirituality and esoteric knowledge.

Jesus even gave us a clue when he said, 'These things that I do, you will do and more.' And yet, so many people close their eyes and their minds to the information we give you to help you progress as Jesus suggested.
To help you progress as Jesus did, we need to study.

Don't forget that the master Jesus started off just like you - an ordinary person.

It was only by long years spent in the Heavenly spheres before incarnating here, studying both spirituality and the way life is created, that turned him into the master you know.

The biblical concept that Jesus was a special, almost angelic being, is false information created to produce an unbridgeable gap between you, then Jesus and God.

Jesus is a person like you and, like you, spent long years developing into the wonderful being he became.

In many cases he studied books similar, if not identical, to the ones we present to you.

Do not think that because Jesus incarnated 2000 years ago that he had access to information different to what you are getting, nor think that Jesus was born a "special" person.
He became special because of his dedication to learning.

It may be a sobering thought that the same - or very similar - books we give you to study, Jesus also studied.
Perhaps it will give you some idea of the importance of the information we give you.
If it helped Jesus to advance to become who he was, and is, perhaps you can understand that, if you study also, you can make his statement that you can become like him come true!

If you had the ability to enter the Akashic Record, and contacted the file in which the life of Jesus is contained, you would see him as a young spirit in the Heavenly spheres, studying at the feet of Masters, who asked him to read and digest exactly the same information that we present to you.
Obviously, with time, he was able to read more advanced books that, so far, we have not been able to present to you but we hope that, eventually, we will be able to publish enough to allow you to have access to all the information that Jesus studied and thus will give you the opportunity to make his wish come true.

Jesus prayed to God, thanking God for the life that he had been given. He meditated, and still does, and he studied the books made available to him.

If you wish to follow in the footsteps of the master Jesus, we suggest you do the same.
Thank God for the life he has given you.
Meditate and study, carefully, the books and other information we give you and there will be nothing preventing you to advance as Jesus advanced.

While we are talking about the life of the young spirit you know as Jesus, please do not think that he was alone studying with his teachers.
In the Akashic Record you would see a whole group of young spirits studying along with Jesus.

It just happened that Jesus decided to incarnate and some others did not, but heaven contains a large number of people who are very wise indeed and are, themselves, creators of Spiritual Law, as Jesus became.

So, we hope that you can realize the importance of the information we have been asked to make available to you.

For those who can accept what we have said above, we hope that this will spur you to greater efforts.

For those who feel shocked, insulted and outraged to imagine any link between the master Jesus and you on Earth at the moment, we must say that we understand and appreciate your difficulties.

However, we are obliged to present truth as we know it to be and if it offends some, we cannot take back truth.

Life as it is presented on Earth at the moment is so full of lies and false information, that it will be difficult for some to break through that barrier.

Thus, they will be denying themselves the chance to progress as Ascension progresses.

However, we make this information freely available to all and it is up to each individual to accept or reject.

For those who cannot release the shackles of false information given for so long, we leave you to live as you choose.
For those who want to Ascend, we bid you welcome.

But, having said all that, let us return to the subject of this book - DNA.

You may remember, that we were discussing how life is constructed, second by second.

Now, what has this got to do with DNA, although we did mention that in the gap where, apparently, nothing exists, DNA was altered?

So, we appear to have two sorts of DNA, not counting the physical sort, that will make a third.
The first is the sort that we have described that contributes to the personality of a person and the second is the type that is present during the momentary gap where all is destroyed.

Now, why should DNA be present at that moment and, if nothing exists, where does it come from?

Obviously, if the Archangels alter the DNA of everything during the brief interlude between two snapshots, then DNA must be present.
We wish you fully to appreciate that the DNA of everything, everywhere, is altered during that infinitesimal moment between any two snapshots of existence, or at least, if not altered, it is examined to assess whether it needs to be altered in order to keep all life in balance.

So, we question how it is possible for so much to be achieved in such a small space of time?
Even though we know that time really doesn't exist, it is still quite a feat to examine and modify the DNA of everything, every living object and creature in such a short moment.

So, we introduce you to yet another aspect of life, hitherto unknown. There is an area where life is contained in a sort of bubble that is outside of time and space, outside of anything previously discussed, that cannot be destroyed when all life is eradicated between any two snapshots.

In fact, this bubble contains the blueprint of existence.

What does that mean and where in all the dimensions is this bubble contained?

First let us apologise for using the word bubble, because it is not a bubble but is information contained in a closed area, remote from anything known to humanity incarnate at the moment.
So, we will continue to use the word bubble and hope that you will be able to appreciate that we are actually talking about a selection of facts, of events that are grouped together by gravity to keep it remote from anything else.

We could have used the word valise (suitcase), backpack or any other term that will enable you to visualize a number of things kept apart from any other things.

So, let us first try to describe where this bubble is situated and then we will see what the bubble contains.

So far, we have described to you eight dimensions or auras, depending on how you look at them, and said that virtually all life as we know it is contained in one of the countless subdivisions of each dimension.
We also mentioned the special place at the end of each dimension reserved exclusively for God and used the example of a long playing record, the last track left blank for God.

We mentioned that the only dimension that was left blank was what is termed the third dimension and every aspect of life is contained in one of the other dimensions, often with connections to another dimension and, finally, we mentioned that DNA is somewhat free to wander about so that it can influence life in whatever way it chooses.

It is this last aspect that gives us a clue to what this bubble is.

There is an area of life that is remote from, outside of, all the eight dimensions.
It is free to wander about, influencing whatever dimension it feels needs help or attention, so it is not actually connected to the eight dimensions, although it is constantly in touch with them.

We are going to use a very simple and almost insulting example to demonstrate in simple terms what we are referring to.

Imagine an office block with eight floors, one on top of another and each floor full of office workers beavering away at computers, holding meetings, etc.
Now imagine a tea lady going from floor to floor offering cups of tea or biscuits or whatever the office workers needed.

We do apologize for using such a childish description and we hope that you won't feel insulted, but if you can understand that, in the example of the tea lady, she goes from floor to floor helping the workers on those floors but, herself, is not in any way connected to the work the office workers are involved with but, at the same time, is helping those workers, you will have understood the principle.

The main difference is, of course, that our tea lady is, in fact, this bubble we referred to and instead of tea and biscuits, spiritual advice is given.

There is much more than just spiritual advice available but we don't have language to describe a bubble of life, able to give help in any dimension and in any form required.

So, let us make it quite clear. This bubble is able to go to any dimension that requires help and to offer that help but is, itself, outside of any dimension.

Whereas our helpful tea lady, when her task is finished, would return to a kitchen area to wash up her teapots and to store her trolley, our bubble has nowhere to rest, so to speak.
It is constantly on the move up-and-down the dimensions and never stops, so it has no "home" as such.

We hope we have made this point clear concerning this bubble of "energy", for want of a better word, constantly on the alert to go to any dimension and to help out with any problem.

You may remember that we said that this bubble contains the blueprint of life.

What does that mean?

One would think that any connection between a grain of sand, a plant, an animal, a human or a galaxy would be minimal but, if you allow that all is one, they are all actually the same thing.

This is a part of existence that is very difficult to appreciate because, obviously, to our eyes, to our senses, there is a vast difference between all things and, as we have said elsewhere, museums are full of items carefully marked so as to denote the difference between various aspects of life and a number of anthropologists and scientists have spent their careers studying these differences and noting in books and essays the non-connections of various objects.

This flies in the face of the statement we make that all is one.
We can't have it both ways - all is one or all is separate - or can we?

It depends, of course, on how one regards things.

Certainly, if we just look at everyday objects with the naked eye, so to speak, there does appear to be countless different stones, plants, animals and humans, not to mention countless galaxies seen through telescopes in the night sky, but if we could switch on our spiritual aspects we could - not exactly see - but feel, appreciate that all is one.

Some fortunate people have had the experience of seemingly being taken to an area outside of Earth and have had their senses bombarded with the knowledge that all is connected, all is one.
In these rare experiences, these lucky people describe being aware of every grain of sand as a living object, of every plant, creature, human and the whole multiverse connected as one.

Is there any connection to that experience and this bubble of existence we mentioned?

Obviously, assuming what some people experience, the answer is yes.

This blueprint, as we described it, is created by the Archangelic beings we have often mentioned that work for the God power and is contained in this bubble.

Is there anything else in the bubble apart from the blueprint for life?

Once again, we must get into deep waters and tell you that there is a special aspect of DNA, quite separate from any other form of DNA that works in close conjunction with this blueprint.

Obviously, for you to understand to what we allude, we need to try to investigate this bubble and the way it works assisting and altering life.

We will repeat, once again, if we may, that all life everywhere, in every part of the multiverse, is like a giant cosmic cine camera, taking endless still snapshots of life and in between any two shots, any two frames, there is a moment when all life ceases to exist.

Life actually exists as we know it and see it to be because of the God Force, working through the power of the Archangels creating everything.

Everything that exists throughout the whole multiverse and throughout all time does so because of the creative power of these incredible Archangels.

As we have said, they make all this so that prime creator, God, can gain experience.

But, the Archangels quickly realised that life (existence) couldn't progress in a smooth line, starting at one point and progressing through time, so to speak, to a point in the future when God decides he has learnt enough and everything stops.

This would have been easiest but, unfortunately, life is always on a balance, swinging back and forth between progress and decline, growth and decay.

Therefore, it was deemed necessary to invent a system where life could be examined periodically and any adjustments made if necessary.

This is because the natural progression of things is towards decay - entropy as it is termed.
We have often mentioned this and have used the example of building a new house. We said that it was necessary, constantly, to maintain the house or it would quickly fall into decay.

This process, in turn, was necessary to invent because, as once again we have often said, if life lived forever in perfect health or condition, soon the whole world would be choked with people, plants, animals, and life would be untenable.
So, it was deemed necessary to introduce negative forces, Angels of Destruction, to act as the trashmen of life and clear up unwanted things.

Births and deaths in physical terms was invented.
Angels of Construction and Destruction were invented, but it was found necessary to invent, also, a system of examination and control to try to keep life in balance.

Therefore, the Archangels invented this cinematic type of system, where life is constructed as a series of small, still frames, and in between any two frames, a system of modifying the life/death process of all things could be manipulated.

Thus, something we call DNA was invented to help with the building/destruction of all things.

If you have ever wondered why people grow from tiny babies to maturity and then start to decline to old age and, finally, death of the physical body, it is DNA (junk DNA) that controls it all.

Obviously, there is more to the story than that. People that abuse their bodies tend to live a far shorter time than people who care for their bodies, but even in those cases, it is DNA that assists in the decline.

But to return to this bubble.

Contained inside this bubble, is the life plan of every object, no matter what it is, and also in the bubble is a special form of DNA.
So, in the brief moment when all life is extinguished, the bubble survives and the life plan of everything is examined by the Archangels and the DNA instructed to alter the so-called junk DNA, so that something either advances or declines, grows or decays according to the life plan.

Once again this is very difficult to appreciate.

For everything, from every grain of sand up to the whole multiverse is monitored and changed, if necessary, billions of times a second according to the life plan of each object and the change is effected by this special type of DNA.

If nothing exists, how can even the special type of DNA affect change in things that do not exist?

What happens is that the life plan of each object is examined and instructions sent to the DNA in the bubble to make the necessary change in whatever it is attached to.
Then, as life comes into being again, that DNA in the bubble sends, telepathically, instructions to the DNA in the non-physical aspect of that object, and as that object starts to reappear, so the change is made.

Now, as this is all happening billions of times a second, it would seem unlikely that there would be time to do anything but, as time is an illusion, in fact, if we could imagine the reappearance in slow motion, the snapshot would appear slowly and so this junk DNA has time to affect the necessary change before life is once again extinguished and the whole process is repeated.

It must be appreciated that each change is very small, but as the small change happens billions of times a second, over time, change occurs.

So, to recapitulate. In the microsecond where life no longer is, the life plan of each object, no matter what it is, remembers the entity that it is attached to, tells the DNA in the bubble to effect a certain change and the DNA in the bubble links with the DNA of the object or entity as it reappears and that DNA makes a small change to the object or entity.

So, it is the life plan within the bubble that, in effect, recreates, through DNA, the object much as it was but with slight change to the DNA.

This life plan is, of course, connected to Higher Self but, from the point of view of this explanation, is also connected to the Archangels, who ordered its creation in the first place.

The question that still remains to be answered is why is this change necessary?

The answer is contained within the curiosity of God.
If there were no changes to anything, life would stagnate and God would not learn.

So, God instructed the Archangels to effect change to all life, slowly, invisibly but inevitably.

Thus it is, that the cycle of life is in constant movement and this movement requires all things to change in order to keep up with this constant change.

So, as life changes slowly, the same Archangels tell the life plan of all things to effectuate change and so the scenario we just described occurs.

All this is done so that prime creator - God - can learn from this process and the experiences that change produces.

It is thanks to this constant change that life exists as it does, both good and bad.

We must also say at this point that what we have described above is also linked to this pendulum swing of life from darkness into light, from descent to ascension.

For those who are not aware of this last event, we are gradually moving into an exciting and wonderful period which will last a vast amount of time. A time we call Ascension, where all people will make a choice. Either to accept Ascension and become better, more spiritual people, or to remain as they are and will still live in darkness.
For those who Ascend, their DNA will change to take account of the increased, positive vibrations entering our bodies and our bodies will gradually change and will start to glow with spiritual power.

For those who remain behind, there will be little or no change.
The life plan and bubble DNA will not bring any advanced change to them.

So, we hope that you can see how complex and intertwined all aspects of life are.

We also hope that you can see the amazing role that DNA plays in the construction and evolution of life.

We will end this chapter here by reminding you that the information concerning this bubble of life plan, plus the special DNA, has never been revealed to man incarnate before, which gives you some idea of how much trust we put in your ability to comprehend and how much you have advanced in recent years.
Up till now, it would have been quite impossible for man to accept this information, but we put our hopes in those of you who are ascending to be able to understand, because this is difficult and advanced spiritual physics we present to you.

In the next chapter we will look at DNA from an even more global aspect.

CHAPTER 7

UNIVERSAL DNA

We now turn our attention to globality, if you will forgive this somewhat uncouth word. What we mean is that, so far, we have concentrated our efforts on how DNA is involved with individual life, no matter what it is, both in physical and non-physical form.

But, of course, there is much more to DNA then we have already explained, even though we hope you will agree that we have explained aspects of DNA hitherto unknown to man incarnate.
We will just add, that there are whole groups of people in the Heavenly spheres that do not interest themselves in esoteric matters and just pass their time in idle pursuits.

The knowledge we impart to you is available to all in the Heavenly spheres, but no one is forced to learn, so there are vast numbers of people who have lived in non-incarnation for long periods of time, who know little more than when they left incarnation.
This is unfortunate, as Ascension is open to all and if people in the Heavenly spheres wish to rise in spirituality, they too, like all of us, must pick up the reins of progression, study, meditate and thank God, or they will forever remain at the level that they currently find themselves.

As we have mentioned, knowledge of aspects of creation is also necessary and is an integral part of the Ascension process.

You may find it strange to hear us say that there are people in Heaven who are not ascended.
We are taught, when in incarnation, that all good people, once they get to Heaven, rise to be one with God.

Nothing could be further from the truth.

Whilst it is true that death brings liberation from the trials and tribulations of incarnation, it does not in any way suddenly provide us with infinite spiritual abilities and infinite knowledge.

When our incarnation ends, we find ourselves at exactly the same point in terms of our spirituality and knowledge, as we were when we finally closed our eyes on Earth.

Spirituality has to be developed in Heaven, in exactly the same fashion as it does on Earth.
Knowledge has to be obtained by study, in exactly the same manner as it does on Earth.

Now, the important point about Ascension is that it gives everyone, both incarnate and discarnate, the opportunity to join together, in a higher elevation of life.

We would like to explain this.

At the moment, people on Earth are, generally, at a fairly low level of spirituality and at a low level of esoteric knowledge.

Even the most devout religious person on Earth is handicapped by the religion to which he belongs and his lack of knowledge about existence.
Even the most educated of professors, if he does not understand esoteric wisdom must, unfortunately, be considered ignorant of the real, meaningful facts of life.

This is why we encourage you to take up meditation, and information about how to do this safely and correctly has been placed on our site by those kind people who give their time to assist us.

Equally, we have spent a number of years providing you with books and lessons revealing the esoteric world to you, information - as we said - that is the exact same, or nearly so, information that people study in Heaven.

The only difference between what you can read and what those studying in Heaven read is that, in the books destined to be read by you, incarnate, we inject passages to help you understand. Information that would not be necessary to those in Heaven.
For instance, the beginning of this chapter, so far, would not be necessary for those in Heaven, so would not be included but we feel, in order to help you understand, that it is necessary to interject short passages of extra explanation to you. But, apart from that the books are identical.

As we said, this information has been studied by generations of students in Heaven because truth does not alter, nor will it ever.
What was true at the beginning will always be true. So, assuming that you walk the spiritual path and, assuming you study the information we give you, you will gradually rise to be of the same level of spiritual development as many people in the Heavenly spheres, who are also meditating, studying and rising in spirituality.

Now, the amazing thing will be that many of you, as you will be at the same level (those incarnate and those discarnate), you will begin vibrating at the same frequency and so, in a way, the barrier between you will break down and you will be able to communicate.

This information has been kept from you for long generations.

There are a number of reasons for this.
1st, whilst the pendulum swing was in negativity, such progress was impossible.

2nd, religions, horrified to think that you, one day, would be able to contact us in Heaven and share information, thus demonstrating that religions are not necessary and would, therefore, lose their grasp on you, have vilified any communication between the two areas, Earth and Heaven, despite there being ample evidence that people like the Master Jesus was in constant communication with Heaven.

3rd, the Archons, also terrified of losing their stranglehold on you, have done their best to prevent any spiritual growth on Earth.

However, Ascension is happening and, if you follow the spiritual path and if you study esoteric wisdom - all of which we explain to you just as it is explained to your friends in Heaven - both groups will rise to the same higher level, at which point, by the Law of Mutual Attraction and by the fact that both groups will be vibrating at this higher level, you will both be able to meet and share information.

Heaven and Earth will, in a fashion, combine.

This may sound fantastic now but we are able to demonstrate this by the simple fact that you are reading this book which is transmitted to our instrument on Earth by the simple fact of joining vibrations.

If we can do this, so as to provide you with information, you, too, can do it.
What one can do, all can do!

It is a question of meditation and development.

We are also training others to develop this skill, but you can do it on your own if you so desire.

As you start to meditate, you will draw towards you guides and helpers who will assist you to develop.

It may take a long time. Spiritual development and the acquisition of wisdom is no slim affair.

But, with patience and with faith and courage it can be done.

You may be wondering why we mentioned this when we are supposed to be talking about DNA?

Those of you who have carefully read the beginning of this book and have understood it, should have noticed that we likened DNA in a personal, individual sense to DNA in a more linked fashion and implied that all humanity is joined together through DNA, or rather, specific aspects of it.

We further implied that, not only has each atom, indeed, each particle within that atom, not only the life spirit but has auras, access (although rather limited) to Higher Self, and all the other attributes that apply to living things, but each particle of each atom, and each atom itself has DNA. This is because all is one.

If something is alive, it must, despite its external appearance, be one with everything else.
It is only personality - Ego - that makes one thing feel separate from another.

Now, if we take this concept on, it implies that the whole galaxy, the whole universe, the whole multiverse must have DNA.

Obviously, this type of DNA is quite different to the DNA we have described before.

Just to remind you, we spoke of the DNA that scientists use to condemn criminals.
We spoke of the miraculous and far-reaching junk DNA and we spoke of "bubble" DNA.

Now we must introduce you to yet another type of DNA that we will call "universal" DNA.

This is perhaps not the best term because it is more than universal, covering all aspects of life to the furthest reaches of the galaxy and beyond.

However, if by "universal DNA" you can appreciate that we refer to a type of DNA that has, so far, not been spoken of by us - nor by anyone else in modern times since the last Extermination Level Event (ELE) - we hope that you can appreciate that we refer to DNA in the most global sense possible.

That is not to say that there are not other versions of DNA, but let us examine universal DNA.

Perhaps we should explain what we mean by universal DNA, before going on to examining and explaining it in detail.

As we mentioned above, as all is one, any attribute that any one thing has, all must have, therefore, from the tiniest living object imaginable, to the greatest, if one has DNA, all must have.

But, you will have noticed that DNA is not quite the same for all things.
Although we refer to these different types of living aspects as DNA, some of them are so different from others as to be an almost separate form of life.
But, no matter how different they might seem, these aspects are, nevertheless, DNA.

One could use as an example, animals or plants. There are such a variety of these things that it is sometimes difficult to accept that they are animals or plants but, despite their different appearances, they are all animals or plants.

It is the same with DNA. There are differences depending on what use the DNA serves but DNA is still DNA.

Now, we will attempt to describe why universal DNA exists.

Quite simply, as all is one, that which applies to the life forms that we have previously described, must apply to life everywhere.

Perhaps we should explain, once again, that everything is alive - with the exception of robots and Artificial Intelligence (A.I.).

All alien life is alive, although their created robots are not.
All angelic forms - both good and evil - are alive.
All planets, all suns, all of space is alive.
We could even stretch this to say that even time is alive, although time is a relative concept.

But if something exists and was created by the Archangelic beings that work for God, it will have a life Logos attributed to it and thus is alive.

In fact, with the exception of robots, machines, A.I. and a few other created objects, all that exists is alive.

So, if virtually everything is alive, as all is one, everything will have DNA, as well as access to Higher Self, Imagination, etc.

It is not easy to imagine that space is alive, that time is alive and, as such, has all the attributes that you have, but it is so.

Anything and everything created by God's Archangels is, at its base, identical. Therefore, the attributes you have, even time and space have, including auras and DNA.

We do appreciate that something as abstract as time is alive, is hard to believe, especially as we have often mentioned that time is an illusion. And so, it is, but like so many things, time might not have any reality in all dimensions, but in the world in which you live, it is very real indeed and life as you know it would be chaotic if you did not have some means of measuring time.

After all, if you think about it, your physical body that you use during your incarnation is an illusion but that does not stop you from having DNA.

So, time, in your reality is real and thus has DNA.

Even in the other types of life (the Heavenly spheres, for example) although we do not use time as you do, we do have sequence of events, one thing happening after another, which is another way of considering time. So, in other dimensions, sequence of events has DNA.

We are entering aspects of creation now that have seldom, or never before, been mentioned

Have you ever heard of anyone saying that time is alive?
Have you ever heard of anyone saying that space is alive?
We could go on and consider other things, like gravity for instance. Gravity is also alive.

We do not want to wander too far from the prime topic of this book which is DNA but it is worth spending a few minutes to try to understand why space, time, gravity and a number of other things are alive.

Time is measurable with clocks but you cannot see time. You can measure its effects but you cannot take time and hold it in your hand.
In fact, the only means we have of knowing that time exists is to measure its passage.

The same would apply to space.
By its very nature, one can measure the distance between two objects but one cannot see or hold in one's hand, space.

Gravity is yet another example.
We can measure its effect but we cannot see gravity.
It is just as well that gravity exists, or all life would shoot off into space as the planet Earth spins!

Electricity is yet another example. We can see a spark. We can measure volts, amperes, etc., but we cannot see electricity, only its effects.

We have somewhat labored the point, but we want you to be aware that there are a number of aspects of life that exist but cannot be observed yet, nevertheless, are part of life, are alive and thus have DNA.

So, we wish you to appreciate that there is life in many areas, some visible, some not.

We have mentioned in another book about the whole of your galaxy being held together by gravity that, basically, forms a sort of gigantic sphere around the exterior of the galaxy holding it together.

We will repeat this in different words.

Already, it is almost impossible for anyone to visualize the galaxy in which you live, so vast is it but, nevertheless, try to imagine the galaxy encased in a transparent globe.

The object of this globe is two-fold.

1st, to make sure that all the planets and suns in the galaxy stay within boundaries.

2nd, as there are other galaxies in the universe, also contained within their sphere of gravity, the gravity makes sure that each galaxy is kept separate from any other galaxy.

Should this not be the case and one galaxy bumped into another, the resulting explosion would be devastating.
Such an event would cause an ELE on a truly universal scale and so the Archangels who construct everything, coat each galaxy with an external sphere of thick gravity, ensuring that no one galaxy would bump into another.

Now, this is where we enter another difficult to understand area of existence.

If you can visualize countless galaxies floating in space, each one contained within a sphere of gravity, logic would dictate that there might be some force controlling and directing these galaxies to behave themselves, if you will pardon our humor.

What we mean, is that some force tells each galaxy to wander about, but to do so in a controlled fashion, so as to avoid any one galaxy from bumping into another.

The question is, of course, what is this force, this intelligence that organizes the whole universe?
The answer is DNA.
In space and in every planet, every sun, is a sort of galactic DNA.
This is the DNA that we have termed "universal DNA" earlier on.

As we have said, DNA is alive but is not really a consciousness as you are or as an angel is.
It is programmed, if one can use that term, to do specific things.

In the case of universal DNA, it is programmed to keep the whole universe - and we mean this in the sense of all of creation, no matter how many light years it might be from us - in order.

It does not necessarily affect any planet or sun directly.
Its job is to keep all in order.

Now, we could ask where this universal DNA is?

The answer is that there is everywhere in the cosmos, what we call "space".
As we have said, space is alive. Therefore, there is in space, life!
There are atoms, sometimes referred to as dark energy, that science has only recently began to investigate.

Dark energy, is quite simply atoms that vibrate to a different frequency to any atom on Earth or, indeed, any planet or sun in the universe.

But dark energy, being made of countless atoms, and each atom being alive, has all the attributes that all life has and thus has DNA.

This DNA is also on a different frequency to anything physical.

If we call "space", full of atoms known as dark energy, one could call this DNA "dark DNA" as it is of the same frequency of so-called dark energy.

However, dark DNA sounds a bit negative so we refer to it as universal DNA.

If you could possibly imagine the amount of space in the whole of existence, you would realize the incredible number of dark atoms there are in space.
As each one of these atoms contains DNA, we can get some idea of the amount of DNA there is in space.

There is sufficient DNA as to be able to use its pre-programming to do its job, which is to keep the whole universe in balance.

We will just wander from the topic of DNA for a moment to talk about supernovas and red giants, etc.

As all is one, a sun must be born, grow to maturity, decline and finally disappear.

Although, as we have said, a sun is a sort of portal, broadcasting energy in the form of frequencies to all the planets that circumnavigate any sun, it has to follow the pattern of all life.

Suns can, and are, being born and others are in the process of coming to the end of their lives.

When this happens, usually the sun will try to draw into itself, the various planets that it has been attached to, so as to not abandon them to their fate and then, finally, it will cease to exist and may remain as a white dwarf for a while.

This white dwarf is, in fact, simply the etheric double of the sun and will dissipate over time.

But, to return to this universal DNA.
We hope you can fully appreciate there is no part of anywhere in physical, and non-physical existence, that some form of DNA is not playing an essential role in helping to keep life in order.

This is because of something called a life plan.

We have explained to you that you have a life plan and that you have your personal DNA that aids you in allowing your life plan to guide you through your incarnation.
It is not hard to accept this.

But what may be more difficult to appreciate is that the whole, mighty, ever reaching universe also has a life plan, and yet, if all is one and all is the same, if you have a life plan, the universe has a life plan.

What its life plan is, is not our concern.
What is our concern is to understand that universal DNA is fully aware of the universe's life plan and is constantly at work implementing it.

It is also worth bearing in mind that the universe has all the attributes you have, which is to say the auras, access to Higher Self, Imagination, ID and all the rest of the things applicable to you, including eight versions of itself.

One would hardly think that the universe would need these attributes but it is as alive as you are - in its own way - and is able to think and make decisions just as you can.

We must never forget that all is one and it is only the universe's Ego (and yours) that make you feel apart.

It would also seem ridiculous to think that a universe can think and make decisions, be influenced by its life plan to make certain changes, but it is so.

We are used to looking into the night sky and seeing various constellations that have been spoken about for many years but it is the fact that the universe operates on a different time scale to you that seems to make the universe appear lifeless.

A day in your life might last a million years to the universe.
But, nevertheless, the universe is alive and, thanks to its DNA and thanks to its life plan, it can, and does, make changes, changes that are too spread out over time as we know it, to make appear real.

Which takes us onto another chapter, which will be about time.

CHAPTER 8

DNA & TIME

Time has always been considered to be something that advances from now to the future in a straight line.

The past can be noted, if not to the day, but possibly to the year (usually) or at least noted as an event that occurred at a certain 'time' in the past and the number of years between an event and the 'now' moment, when we are considering the event, can be calculated. Thus, making a smooth transition from the past until now.

Even the future can be noted with precision.

Governments and business houses plan into the future and declare that such and such an event will come to fruition at some date in the future.

So, looking at time from that point of view, there is not much to discuss.
It seems fixed and, if you will excuse us for using a somewhat mocking expression, is part of the point of view that, 'God is in his heaven and all's right with the world.'

The problem is, as we have gone to great lengths to explain to you, life is seldom as simple as it seems.

Certainly, we would agree that God is in his heaven and all's right with the world, but that is not because we have a comprehension and control of all things, but just because it is true that God exists and all will always unfold according to predetermined life plans, so all must be right with the world, no matter what actually happens.

But we wish to present to you a different way of regarding time.

If we go back to the distant past when humanity was in its caveman phase, time was unknown.

The only means of noting time was that planet Earth was flooded with light as the sun rose and then the light disappeared, darkness came and early man retired to their caves for shelter.
Before fire was invented, we presume they slept, but once fire was discovered, the cavemen could prolong the waking period by using fire as an artificial light.

As an interesting aside, it has always been assumed that cavemen had no sophisticated language, but if one imagines a family in a cave or shelter of some kind, sitting around a fire, what did they do? Sit, looking into the flames and twiddling their thumbs or were they able to discuss things?

We rather feel that they had sufficient language to discuss matters of moment and pith to them.

Perhaps they could not discuss the finer points of philosophy but we think that they had sufficient language to discuss the day's hunting, what worked and what did not, and discuss the next day's hunting and other topics important to them.

It seems to us that one of the difficulties that have kept animals from developing is their lack of language.
Exchanging thoughts by speaking is of great importance in developing.

Those able to use telepathy may communicate, of course, but it is helpful, even when using telepathy, to have a language in order to convey thoughts.

For example, these books appear, thanks to telepathy, between us in the Heavenly spheres and an instrument incarnate on Earth, but you will notice that it is all based around words - not just exchanging thoughts.

So, we wonder if primitive man had not developed speech much earlier than is supposed?

However, this has little connection to our discussion about time although, as there is actually only the "now" moment, it does have some relevance.

Let us not complicate issues, but try to describe what we know about time.

We think you will agree that, in your reality, to be able to calculate time is of great importance and modern life would be totally untenable without clocks telling us that we have to do certain things at certain moments.
In our reality, of course, we have no need of clocks, although those of us that communicate regularly with people incarnate are aware of your time and prepare ourselves to communicate with our colleagues incarnate at times that we know the person on Earth is also getting ready to communicate with us.

We would not expect, for instance, communication with someone incarnate in the middle of the night, when the earthly instrument is asleep, nor when the person is at his place of employment.

So, although we do not use time as such, always being in the "now" moment, we are aware of time when we interrelate with you incarnate.

Therefore, we hope that you can see that time really only applies to you on Earth.

It is considered to be a scientific rule, that if some concept is not true in all cases, it cannot be accepted as fact.

In which case, we can say that time is not a scientific fact, although it is used by virtually all people all the time.

Scientists use time in very precise ways in order to make certain scientific instruments operate and try to make sense of the world in which you live.

Indeed, without using crystals that vibrate at certain frequencies and that can be used to create clocks of various kinds, you would not have computers, satellites and many of the tools that you use that have electronic components in them.
Even modern microwave cookers, washing machines, dryers, cooking ovens, etc., have electronic devices in them to enable you to program them precisely.

All this is connected to time.

So, we appear to have a problem, a dichotomy.
On one hand, we have scientific law that states if something is not true in all cases it cannot be accepted as scientific truth - and we have said that only you, incarnate, use time - and at the same time, we have scientists using time to manufacturer virtually everything that exists nowadays.

There are a surprising number of objects manufactured today that contain computerized elements and most of these have a clock system controlling the electronics.

Of course, science ignores the non-physical aspects of life, for the moment, and so does not see the problem.

However, in the future, scientists will be forced to accept that life outside of physicality exists and, once again, Pandora's Box will be opened to try to balance physicality with non-physicality.

Of course, we will be there, ready and willing to assist science in taking this leap of faith into accepting true life into the somewhat artificial life that physicality denotes, and we will assist as best we can in helping science to bridge the psychological gap between what has been accepted as the limit of physics and the fact that there is a whole world of new physics (not new, but new to them) that will be made available.

Accepting that aliens exist will aid in mind expansion, as well understanding immortality.

Therefore, as you can already see, time is more complicated than appears at first sight.

We have, on one hand, time as measured on Earth and time - if we can consider sequence of events as time - in the non-physical dimensions.

In order to make sense of time, we need to find some means of linking the two ways of considering time so that the word fits both aspects.

Let us really consider what we know about time.

We would agree that physical life operates using clocks, and even people that live in remote areas and don't have watches, use the sun as a measuring device and are thus aware of the passage of time.

But, at the same time, in physicality, we don't need to have our eyes glued to a clock to inform us of certain events.

Certainly, if we need to get to our employment at a certain time each day, or need to catch a train or an aeroplane, we need to keep a close eye on time, but at weekends, holiday times or for those who do not work, usually, time is of less importance.
At such times, generally, the person rises from bed when he feels like getting up, prepares himself for the day, has his breakfast and passes the day without following a ritual timed to the minute.

It is only those who are actively employed in the cogs of industry and enterprise that follow time by the clock.

Those we mentioned above, people not working, use sequence of events; rising, preparing themselves, having breakfast, etc.

Whatever time of the day that these people perform these acts, it is the fact that they are performed that is important, not the precise moment as measured by a clock that they take place.

If ever mankind progressed to the point that no one worked, time would lose a lot of its importance.

We mention this to help you realize that even for those who work for a living and, thus, have to perform the rising ritual at precise moments to ensure that they arrive at their employment at a precise time are, in fact, following the sequence of events pattern, but they are combining time with the sequence of events.

Many, if they follow this sequence for enough years, start to use what is called their "biological clock" and scarcely have to look at a physical clock. The rising ritual is so ingrained within them that they always - or nearly always - manage to arrive at their employment in an almost mechanical way.

The biological clock is of great importance and we will discuss this at great length later.

But let us first try to finish our discussion of time versus sequence of events.

We know that most people must rise at a certain time and many have an alarm clock to arouse them.

But we are sure that many of you also tend to wake up at that precise moment. Your biological clock has learnt to wake you up at the same moment each working day. The alarm clock only acts as a safeguard or to help you if you have had a late night or something.

From that moment, by experience, you know just how long you can spend preparing yourself, eating breakfast, getting to work, etc., so as to arrive at your employment at the requisite time.

Once again, these actions become automatic and the person scarcely needs to look at the clock because he knows intuitively what time it is.

It is only if something disturbs the pattern, that the person has to take note of the time, so as to catch his train or whatever.

So, if someone was asked the sequence of events that he has to follow in the morning and, indeed, throughout the day, he could, more or less, describe his day from experience, as a series of events, that follow on from the moment of rising until the moment of returning to bed at the end of each day.
Obviously, within each event there will be unexpected things that he must deal with but, generally, a person could describe, for instance, arriving at work at a certain time, then coffee break, then lunch break, afternoon tea break, the journey home, evening meal and so on until he retires for the night.

Thus, many people's days are defined by a series of events, one after another.
These events coincide, of course, with certain times that these events are centred around.

Let us explain this in more detail.

A person might be required to start his work day at, say, 7am, 8am, 9am or whatever, followed by a coffee break a few hours later and then lunch break after that.
So, although these events might occur at different times of the day, it is the fact that they occur in sequence that interests us.

Obviously, not everyone's day follows the pattern we have described but, for millions all over the world, they would agree that what we have described fits their work day.
So, we have this combination of sequence of events and the time these events occur.

For many people, the sequence of events refers exclusively to them, depending on how far from their place of employment they live for example and, what specific things they have to do between rising and arriving at their place of employment.

This raises another point.

We have time, sequence of events, but both time and sequence of events are tied to each individual, depending on what his day is filled with.

People are not clones. They are thinking beings who have, according to their life plan, and according to their responsibilities, a number of things, exclusive to them, to do, that alter their time and sequence of events.

Therefore, we wish to introduce to you the concept that time is different for all people.

If you have followed our other teachings, the concept that you have your personal aspect of most, or many things, will not come as a surprise.

Time is presented to us as if it is just one thing, one creation for all people, but a moment's thought should reveal to you that it is personal for all people.

For instance, at the moment that we are dictating this information to our instrument on Earth and he is doing his best to transcribe, accurately, what we say to him, he is of a certain age, sex, lives in a certain house in a certain country and is sitting in a certain room writing these words.
So, according to a large number of factors, this information is being recorded at a certain "time" which includes all the aspects we mentioned above.

But, assuming that this book is eventually made public, you will be reading the same words but under entirely different circumstances.

You may read these words days, weeks, months or years after the scribe is writing them.
You will almost certainly be in a different house, city or country.
You may be male or female, young or old, in good or poor health.
Assuming this book is translated into a different language, you may well not be reading it in the English that we are dictating it in.
In other words, we have a number of aspects of time.
There is the time that this book was first created in the Heavenly spheres, the time that we dictate to our scribe, then the time that you read it.

The meaning behind the words may have different connotations according to the level of comprehension you have.
It will be further modified by your mastery of the language, your mental and emotional state and your previous spiritual education.

This book, this chapter, will be further modified by a whole host of other factors, health, age, the time you have to spare to carefully read the message - or not - and so on.

We have noticed the reaction that we get to the information that we give.

Some people have obviously really understood what we try to explain whilst others have not grasped the meaning at all, a fact we see from the questions asked.

Then, there are those who accept and appreciate what we say whilst others reject the information.

Yet, others have their faith in God strengthened by the message, whilst others are convinced that we are in league with the devil.

All these different points of view spring from the identical information written.

So, if we bring all this together, just concentrating on the words of this chapter, we have a large variety of aspects of time all linked to the same words.

The moment when this was first created in the Heavenly spheres, long ago.
The moment when we could dictate it to our scribe on Earth.
The moment when it was published.
The moment when you discovered it and started to read it.

So, for the same message, a large amount of time factors come into play.

Then, as we said, according to where you live, your sex, your education, your previous beliefs, etc., all this will colour your comprehension and reaction to these words.

So, we hope that you can see that from the same words contained in this chapter, there are a vast number of aspects of time linked to these words, including aspects of your personality.

We will go on to say that your reaction to these words will be colored by all that has happened to you since your birth; birthplace, knowledge of language, level of comprehension, intelligence, level of open mindedness and so on.

So, in effect, the words that you are reading at this precise moment, is the result of a number of time factors that brought the words to your attention, plus a large number of other factors that are, themselves, based on the past that you had, past being an aspect of time.

This is information not easy to understand, because we have linked your birthplace, sex, education and all sorts of personal or personality traits or aspects, to time.

This may not be obvious at first thought, but if you think deeply about what we said, your past (time) affects what you are reading at this exact moment.
Further, all this is related to you and to you alone.

No two people have the same past, the same upbringing, and thus, no two people have the same understanding of these words and yet, the same words are being read by a number of people.
We can only try to make sense of what we are reading now based on what happened to us in the past, our life plan and, basically, who we are.

Therefore, we wish you to try to understand that time and who you are, are linked.

We might use another example.

We are sure that you have all passed moments of great joy, in which case time seems to fly by and, equally, you have passed through moments of great stress, in which case time seems to drag.

The essential point is that time as measured by a clock is not all that time is.

It is also linked to who we are as individuals.

We do realise that some will have difficulty in linking time to personality but for those who can, we wish you to grasp that time is individual for all people.

There is, in fact, no one time as measured by a clock.
That sort of time is just one part, one aspect of time.
Time is individual for all people who have lived, are living or will live.

We mentioned this when we considered history books.

If we could consider something like the rise and fall of the Roman Empire.
Now, we are not referring to any one book because we are sure that there must be a book with that title.
We are referring to the historical fact that the people of Rome spread and conquered a large portion of the world and a large group of people, before being chased away.

But, as we said, to fill a book with facts and figures about how Italian people acted at that time is not really the history of that epoch at all.

The true history would need to describe the complete life history of each and every man, woman and child - even the animals involved - before it could be considered to be a true history of that moment in time.

Once again, this history of that time would need to describe the personalities of all the people involved, thus demonstrating once again, but from a different point of view, that time is personal to each individual.
It is not an account of a few centuries of time, but the experiences and reactions to every person who lived and was affected by the so-called Roman Empire.

Now, why are we going to such lengths to explain all this?

We hope to demonstrate that time is greatly different and vastly more complex than just watching the hands of a clock slowly turning.

We hope, also, that you can see that time is connected to the events people have experienced, are experiencing or will experience in their lives.

It could, of course, be argued that if people didn't exist in physicality, time would have no meaning.

Let us explain this.

Whilst it has been calculated that the planet Earth was formed a certain number of billions of years ago in the past and that the universe was formed several trillions of years ago, there is no real proof to any of this.
It is all speculation by so-called scientific people, who have no real means of calculating the true age of either Earth or the universe.

Then we have Christianity, that has calculated the age of various saints and wise people, it being assumed that one person "begat" another and the result of these calculations is published (in the Bible) and claimed to be a very short period of time that the Earth has existed.

We can say from our somewhat more elevated position, that none of these ages are correct. We will also say that, before man developed sufficient intellect to think of and to try to estimate the age of the Earth and the universe, time had no relevance.

But there was sequence of events and we have discussed this somewhat in relation to caveman.

Even if we examine the way scientists calculate time in relation to experiments or in terms of the vibrations of crystals as used in computers, we inevitably return to the fact that man is involved with the calculation of time.

We suggest to you that time only has relevance when man, past, present or future, is involved in examining it.

From there, no doubt, some of you are already thinking that, as man in nearly all his aspects is connected to DNA, time, as man is involved, will have DNA connected to it in one fashion or another.

Obviously, time, as measured by the hands turning on a clock, will have little or no connection to DNA, but, as the relevance of the passage of time only has any significance when man is involved, we can link DNA to time.

We need to expand on this to make it perfectly clear how time and DNA are connected.

At the risk of repeating what we have already said, about the average person and how his life may be ruled by time, each and every person has much, indeed, most of his character and make up defined by DNA.

This, in turn, influences who he is - male or female, intelligent or not, interested in various things.
In turn, this will influence the way he lives his life, family, employment or leisure.
This, in turn, links his life to the time in which he has to do things and it is all linked to DNA.
Not time, directly, but time as lived by someone.

We hope from the above explanation that you can see that there is, in fact, a link between time as measured by the hands of a clock turning and, by passing through people, DNA.

We wish you also to understand that there is not a specific type of DNA that is connected to time, but is all of the types of DNA that man has, that can be connected to DNA, with the possible exception of the basic type known to man that is used to check blood samples.

It is the other types, connected to the esoteric aspects of humanity, that are brought into play when considering time.

We mentioned that we would be discussing biological clocks, the moments that we have trained ourselves to react to at a certain time.

This term, biological clock, also takes into account animals that do certain things at certain times; mating, migrating and a number of other things.
These acts are done quite unconsciously by both humans and animals.

You must be aware of the effects of DNA sufficiently by now to realize that DNA is behind all these acts, events carried out several times a day or just once a year.

This marvelous and complex chemical/spiritual force is able to count time so as to prod the body to take certain actions when it is the moment.

We have discussed this action already and have likened certain aspects of DNA to an alarm clock and that flags are pre-programmed to go off to inform the body that it is the moment to take certain actions.

We call that alarm clock a biological clock, although it is not DNA that is contained in physicality.
It is astral DNA, associated with the non-physical part of us.

However, its effect is usually felt in both aspects of our make-up; physical and non-physical.

The non-physical part makes us aware of a desire, an unease, a feeling that certain actions should be taken and, usually, it is followed by physical action of some kind.

So, it is not entirely a biological clock. It is both physical and non-physical.

This biological clock is an aspect of DNA that is of considerable importance above and beyond just prodding a few beings to doing things at certain times.

It is closely linked to our life plan and also to Higher Self although, as we have said, there is only one Higher Self for all people and the biological clock is generally considered to be an aspect of each individual. And so, it is.

However, it is far more widespread than that.

We could consider that all of humanity incarnate has a collective biological clock and we could take it on further to stay that planet Earth itself is affected by its version of a biological clock and, indeed, the whole Galaxy is also affected by its own biological clock.

Once again, we remind you that all is one and so what applies to one, applies to all.

If you have a biological clock, everything has a biological clock.

If we leave individuality for the moment and consider the entire human race, there are "waking up" moments, times when virtually the entire population decide to do something.

We will, first and foremost, say that wars are not part of the population's biological clock.

Wars are instigated by Archon controlled people, who consider it necessary to promote wars for various reasons; financial benefit in creating arms of all sorts which are sold to governments at profit and, above all, to create fear, which is food for Archons, then the idea of reducing the world's population, reducing freedom of movement and so on.

None of this has anything to do with biological clocks although, when one sees the ease with which whole nations are persuaded to go to war with each other, it seems like a programmed event.

Biological clocks are DNA that triggers events as mankind progresses.

At the moment, after many millennia of waiting for the universe - indeed, the multiverse - to move into Ascension (another biological clock effect), so whole populations are waking up to the reality of the way that they have been treated, and are protesting.
This is a biological clock effect, that was set up in the collective consciousness long ago by Archangels in order to allow the Ascension process to progress without hinder.

Now, we wish to state to you that biological clocks do not work quite like as an alarm clock does. An alarm clock, especially a digital one, rings at a precise moment, where as a biological clock works rather more slowly.

So, this awakening of the world's population and the elimination of the evil ones, takes place slowly and methodically.

Certain countries are more awake than others, so the awareness of how they have been enslaved happens more rapidly in some countries than in others.

Equally, those countries that are rigidly controlled by Archon influenced religions, will take longer to break free, but this liberation is programmed to occur - indeed, has already started - and will proceed inexorably until all of humanity is freed from Archon control.

If the evil ones could only recognize that this is so and, no matter what they do, their time is over, peace could be obtained so much more easily. This would benefit the evil ones, as the peace and rise in spirituality of the various populations would open the doors to an equitable settlement to the problem and people would find it easy to forgive the evil ones.

But they are struggling and fighting, reluctant to lose face and power.
This will create tension in which some people will wish to harm the evil ones and so a great deal of physical damage may be inflicted on those who are found to be perpetrators of heinous crimes.

It is this awakening time that will be dangerous to the evil ones and the more they try to resist, the more harm they will receive.

It is a bit like a boxing match, in which one contestant is hopelessly outmatched, but continues to fight instead of throwing in the towel.

We are sure that the evil people are aware of the situation, but are so used to having the upper hand, that they are reluctant to throw in the towel.

They are trying by all the means at their disposal to stop, or at least delay, Ascension, but they are fighting a losing battle.

Indeed, the fight is already lost and they would do well to recognise defeat.

Obviously, there are other national and human biological clock effects, such as the increase in the desire to become vegetarian.

Another one is the desire to eliminate poisonous pesticides in food production.

These are all biological clock effects.

There are many more, but you can see for yourself how suddenly, whole populations decide to do something.

Abolishing capital punishment is one, although it still goes on in some places.
Abolishing corporal punishment in schools and prisons is another.

People suddenly decide that something that has existed for long ages is no longer acceptable.
Or suddenly decide to adopt something: Animal Rights springs to mind.
In many countries, hunting is being frowned upon and will eventually be abolished.
Mistreating cats, dogs, horses and other so called "pets" is being banned in many countries.

These are examples of whole populations waking up due to biological clocks and much of what is being introduced today has a connection to Ascension which, as we have said, is a major biological clock awakening call.

Now, it may be difficult to accept that the whole multiverse has a biological clock and DNA, but it is so.

The Pendulum swing that we mentioned is, in effect, the multiverse's biological clock moving us all - and by all we mean everyone in all dimensions - to be flooded with the light of God and it is the DNA of the multiverse that is causing this.

We do appreciate that it is not easy to imagine that planet Earth, the Galaxy and the whole multiverse has DNA but it is so.

All life is one.
Size has no relevance.

Therefore, we feel that we have explained sufficient about DNA in a global sense to give a clear picture of these aspects of DNA, in relation to time, and we'll move on to the next chapter, which will discuss DNA in a more universal state.

CHAPTER 9

DNA IN ILLUSION

We have discussed this incredibly important aspect of existence called DNA and have tried to demonstrate that it is connected to absolutely everything, from the tiniest particle inside an atom, to the whole multiverse, itself and have stated that it is second only to the Logos of God.

This gives some measure of how important we consider it to be, because the Logos of God, contained within the soul, is the stamp of authority from God itself to be alive and to be God.

So, to say that DNA is second only to that gives some idea of how important we consider it to be.

Also, we seem to have covered just about every aspect of DNA, from the physical sort that police and scientists use to compare blood or tissue samples, up to and through the dimensions and have explained this connection, not only to time, but to the biological clock of the universe and the multiverse.

Can there be more to discuss?

Obviously, this is a rhetorical question and the answer is yes.

The problem is that there are areas of existence that are far outside of anything known and so, as these aspects of life would have DNA as an integral part of them, to explain the DNA connection would require a long and detailed explanation of the aspects themselves.

This would take us away from the aims of this book, which is to demonstrate that DNA is closely connected to most aspects of known life.

It is not our desire, in this book, to delve into areas that humanity incarnate has no knowledge of and, as we have said, there are areas of life so difficult to explain that you probably would be baffled by any explanation.

So, we are fast approaching the barrier between what we consider to be possible of comprehension by most people, and the areas that would best be left unsounded for the moment.

Of course, we wish to hide nothing and our aim is to enable all people to understand all aspects of life, but this must be done slowly and carefully, allowing you time to digest what we have already stated.

None of this is helped by the fact that much of what is considered to be known about life is simply not true and so we have to break through the barriers created by false information - to help you unlearn what you believed to be true - before we can replace lies with truth.

We blame religions, partly, for creating fables and we blame science for disseminating false teachings to their students.

However, as we have often stated, times are changing and these Archon created myths about life will be rejected and will be replaced by truth.

The problem we have, as we stated, is to reveal to you, aspects of creation that you already know about through our teachings, as opposed to aspects that have remained outside of your knowledge.

But, we will introduce you to one aspect because, although it will be new to all mankind incarnate, is sufficiently close to what is known as not to be too shocking to you.

Also, the DNA of this new topic is of such importance that, not to mention it, would be to fail in our attempt to describe DNA.

So, we will do our best to describe this new topic in as simple a fashion as possible and hope you will be able to accept it.

Let us, as an introduction, go back and remind you of some of the things we have described in other books that will have relevance to this new topic.

We have stated that all is one, that one is God and, as God is an unknowable force living in "nothing land", so all that you think exists, all that you consider to be real is, in fact, illusion.

The only things that exist are curiosity and imagination.

These two esoteric terms have no physicality; therefore, you have no physicality!

You are just God pretending to be a "something".

Therefore, we have the somewhat unenviable task of moving beyond the illusionary world in which we all live (us in the Heavenly spheres as well as you), and describe how imagination and curiosity can possibly be connected to DNA.

And yet, if what we said about all being one is true, even abstract concepts like imagination and curiosity, if they exist, must have DNA.
If this were not so, this whole book about DNA would be meaningless.

As, we hope, we have satisfactorily argued in favor of DNA in this illusion, and this illusion is created by curiosity and imagination, we may say that both curiosity and imagination must contain DNA.

Indeed, the DNA of curiosity and imagination is of paramount importance in the construction of illusion.

We don't know if we can explain this simply and satisfactorily, but we will try.

Most good stories start at the beginning, go on to the end and then stop. But life is not like that.
It is circular. It is a ring, a ball, a sphere, if it could be visualized.
There is no beginning point.

Imagine the wheel of a cart or a motor car.

It exists and might be made of wood in a horse drawn cart, or metal and rubber in the case of an automobile, but you could not point to a place where it starts nor where it ends.

You could run your hands around it endlessly.

But, if we take a wheel, it serves a purpose.

If we take, for example, a horse drawn cart, as the horse advances, the wheel turns.

If one were a tiny creature sitting on an inside edge of the wheel, as the wheel turns, the little creature might be aware of motion but would possibly perceive that motion as travelling in a straight line.

But if we observe the wheel, we see it turning.

If we look at the tracks made on, say, a muddy road as the cart progresses, we would see a straight line in the mud, very similar to that being experienced on the edge of the wheel by the tiny creature.

So, depending on our point of view, we have two versions of the same motion.
In one case, just looking at the straight line track left in the mud by the passage of the cartwheel, we could imagine that something had been dragged in a line through the mud and anyone looking at the track, if they did not know that wheels exist, could, and probably would, be convinced and argue that something had been dragged through the mud.

Then we have the little creature that would, if he could communicate with us, to a certain extent support the argument of the first person, that an object has moved through the mud, but all this would be contradicted by yet a third person who claimed to have seen a circular wheel and the mark left was made as it rotated, that above the wheel was a cart, a box-like structure, and that a horse had pulled the cart through the mud.

What horse?
No one mentioned a horse!

Out comes a magnifying glass and the track is minutely examined and no evidence of a horse found. Of course, if the gaze of the person examining the track moved a few feet away, he would see the marks left by the horse's hooves, but in the track, there is no evidence about a horse.
Nor is there any evidence of a box-like structure (the cart).
There is just a straight line left in the mud.

Further, if the person who saw the horse and cart from a short distance claims to have seen that the cart was loaded with goods of some nature - bales of hay, sacks of corn or whatever - the story, from the point of view of the person examining the track, would seem to be more and more unlikely.

If there were goods in a cart and a horse pulling the cart along, it would indicate that some person has loaded the cart and that would imply some intelligent life force which, in turn, would imply a connection to DNA through the DNA in the wheel and in the cart, the DNA of the horse, the DNA in the goods being transported and the DNA in the person who loaded the cart.

Now, as all we have to go on is a track in the mud, all the rest of the story can safely be dismissed as illusion.

There is no wheel, no cart, no goods, no horse and no person loading these goods.
There is no evidence and no proof, thus we can safely dismiss the whole story and rest on our laurels.

If the person who really saw the scene keeps on, we can mock him, laugh at him or, as a last resort, shut him up either by locking him in a lunatic asylum or by even more drastic means.

Thus, we remain with this slim evidence of a track in the mud and need look no further.

We present this story to you in order for you to realize that there is more than one way of looking at life.

We can either look at life purely through physical evidence, like looking at the track in the mud, or we could look at life from the more expanded view of the person who saw the horse and cart, or yet again, we can look at life from both aspects and accept that some people have only a limited vision of life, but that also a more expanded view exists.

We suggest to you, if we may, that it would be wise to accept both versions.

If we can pass through life accepting and understanding that some people remain ignorant of expanded wisdom and that they have the right to be like that, even though we might be in possession of greater knowledge, we can live in peace with both factions.

Thus, we live in peace with both them and with ourselves.

We might question what this story has in connection to DNA as it applies to us?

The answer is not easy to explain, but we will try.

We explained to you that the little story about the horse and cart and the track in the mud had two ways of looking at it depending on one's point of view and that DNA was really only connected to the expanded version of it: the wheel, the cart, the horse, the baggage on the cart and the person loading the cart.

But we could prove none of that!

This takes us on to the idea that if nothing exists except curiosity and imagination, even if these things have DNA - a strange form, we will admit - we get the feeling that the story is not complete.

There must, surely, be more to life than just curiosity, imagination and DNA?

This is where we need to make a quantum leap and say that even curiosity and imagination can only exist because there is another force behind these concepts pulling the strings, so to speak.

We are not talking about God, nor his Archangels.

Between these two concepts and us, there are countless other levels of existence totally unknown to man.

As we said, it is not our function, at this time, to explain these levels of existence.
We will only deal with one and that will be hard enough to explain.

We need to try to explain that, between the life we all lead in all dimensions, are an endless number of different lives, different ways of looking at things outside of and beyond any aspect we could really talk about.

We are not referring to alternative realities and we are not referring to any life that could possibly be connected to anything known at the moment.

We are referring to a totally different form of life, far removed from us.
It exists in other areas, other frequencies.

Once again, we are not referring to the kindergarten sphere we investigated in a previous book.
After all, this kindergarten life area is closely connected to our galaxy and our dimensions.
Nor are we talking about life on the other side of nothingness!

This is a place that you could not imagine in your wildest dreams, yet exists, is real and is, in a bizarre fashion, influencing us.

We hope that you can see our problem.

We spoke about physical life and how hard that is to grasp in all dimensions and we spoke about it all being an illusion.
Then we spoke about curiosity and imagination and said that was all that existed - concepts, we think you will agree, that are almost impossible to connect to life as we know it to be - and now we are saying that they only exist because some other area, some other force, totally unknown, that is contributing to the illusion in which we all live.

The problem we have, is that words do not exist to describe this area, nor is there any way of imagining it. It is outside of anything we can grasp.

And yet, we need to try to present it to you because of its DNA.

In fact, if we simplify the concept, we could say that it is the area that creates DNA.
It is actually much more complicated than that, because life, as we will all discover one day, is infinitely complex and we are not sufficiently advanced in esoteric wisdom to be able to comprehend these strange, yet remarkable concepts.

So, to make it as simple as possible, let us just try to imagine and describe the creation area of DNA.

We will say that, if something exists, it has to have been thought of and created somewhere.

So often we just accept that things exist and look no further.

We described this in the horse and cart story where we look at the track left in the mud, accept that it is there, but look no further.

But, of course, if we step back, we see the events that caused the track.

If we had the means, we could take our investigation onwards and describe the horse; stallion or mare, breed, age, etc.
We could ask who made the wheel and visit his place of work, watch him creating wheels, find out what wood is used.

We could talk to the wheelwright and find out if he is married, with children, where he lives and all about the man.

We will stop here this dissertation, but you can see that from a mysterious track in mud lies a vast and complex series of events, of actions, of forms of life, only distantly related to the track in the mud.

But, the point is, if it were not for all these disparate elements coming together, the track in the mud would not have been made.

Up till now, we suggest, science has rather been like someone looking at the track in the mud, just examining what can been seen and totally ignoring all the incredibly complex events that contributed and combined to produce this track.

Equally, all the behind-the-scene events have DNA. Each and every atom of all the elements; wood, iron, fire (furnace), people, clothes, buildings. Each and every thing that contributed to the production of that track contains DNA.

In other words, in a way, if it were not for the overriding importance of DNA, that track would not exist.

We have somewhat labored the point, but we wish to reinforce in your minds, that DNA is of vital importance to the creation of life.

Therefore, we can be sure that the Archangels who work for God and implement all that God desires to be created, thought long and hard about some force, some concept that would need to be created that would, ultimately, produce the multiverse as we now know it to be.

So, they created DNA.

We hope that you can appreciate that DNA is the one, constant factor, that glues all life together into a composite whole.

So, as we said, DNA is second only to the Logos of God itself.

We might almost say that it is its partner, its adiunctus, and without DNA, nothing would exist.

But, DNA needed to be created somewhere.
So, an area was created where DNA could be invented.

Can you imagine that we cannot really describe the process that was used to produce DNA in astral form? In fact, it was created far above the astral planes in areas that we cannot describe and, once perfected, was lowered in frequency into all the dimensions, the sub-dimensions and, finally, into physicality.

All this was created, as and when the various stages of life were also created and, as they were created, DNA was linked to the dimensions and the people and objects in them. DNA helped to solidify and perfect these life forms.

Now, we know that we have not really described this area, nor have we described the processes put into play to create DNA.
We ask you to accept, if you will, that DNA was created by Archangels long ago in an area far remote from anything you are aware of and, gradually introduced to life in the manner that we told you life was placed in, and on, the various dimensions.

Life and DNA go together and we can't have one without the other.

We wish also to inform you, just to whet your appetite, that this area where DNA is invented is only one of a vast number of areas where other aspects of life were/are created.

The unfortunate fact is that, for the moment, we have no means of describing these areas, and if we did, you could not possibly understand, because life is infinitely more complex than what appears, much more complex than anything we have described to you.

It will take generations before mankind will develop to the point that he will be able to imagine these other areas.

If you can accept that life is, indeed, more complex, more diverse than anything imaginable at the moment, that will sow the seeds to, one day, being able to comprehend more about life.

Although this book is not long and although, as always, we have not fully explored all the aspects of DNA, we have presented, we hope, a fairly comprehensive overview of DNA and how important it is in all areas of life.

We hope that you found this book interesting, informative and presented in an understandable fashion.

So, we will finish this book here and select the next one which will take you on to other areas of existence.

We ask the blessing of almighty God on each and every one of you as you progress along the path of Ascension and we send you on wings of angels.

Made in the USA
Las Vegas, NV
28 April 2025